CONTEMPORARY COMMUNITY HEALTH SERIES

FRAGILE FAMILIES, TROUBLED CHILDREN

FRAGILE FAMILIES,

Elizabeth Elmer

CO-INVESTIGATORS:

Sue Evans
John B. Reinhart

TROUBLED CHILDREN

The Aftermath of Infant Trauma

University of Pittsburgh Press

Published by the University of Pittsburgh Press, Pittsburgh, Pa. 15260
Copyright © 1977, University of Pittsburgh Press
Feffer and Simons, Inc., London
Manufactured in the United States of America

Library of Congress Cataloging in Publication Data

Elmer, Elizabeth
  Fragile families, troubled children.

  (Contemporary community health series)
  Bibliography: p. 149
  Includes index.
  1. Child abuse—Longitudinal studies.   2.   Child
development—Longitudinal studies.   I.   Evans, Sue,
joint author.   II.   Reinhart, John B., joint author.
III.   Title.   IV.   Series.
HV713.E5   362.7′1   77-74551
ISBN 0-8229-3351-9

HV
713
.E5

Chapter 2 is an elaboration of "A Follow-up Study of Traumatized Children,"
by Elizabeth Elmer, which appeared in *Pediatrics* 59 (1977):273–79. Used by
permission.

Publication of this book
was made possible by a grant
from the Maurice Falk Medical Fund.

Contents

Tables and Figures

Tables

Figure

Preface

It was only by sheerest chance that I became involved in the activities that would become my chief professional interest. The year was 1957 and I was a social worker at Children's Hospital in Pittsburgh. A physician friend had just finished a session with the house staff concerning the legal aspects of medical practice; the illustrative case was an infant boy of five months who had been admitted to the hospital late the preceding night. The baby was in a coma, had a bulging fontanel, and appeared to have sustained inflicted injuries to the trunk and legs. The young parents had left quickly, before talking with the resident, but the impression of the staff was that the couple were reluctant to discuss their baby and what had happened to him. The baby's condition and the elusiveness of his parents raised questions concerning possible legal issues. For example, if medical personnel should judge the infant abused, what recourse would they have in the law? Should police be called? How could one reconcile the confidential nature of the doctor-patient relationship with the need to involve law enforcement officials? My friend spoke enthusiastically of the interest the case had aroused in the residents concerning the relationship between medicine and the law. "Why don't you go up and see the baby and look over the record?" he remarked. Although he could not remember the family name, the physician felt sure that the head nurse would be able to identify the child from the description that he gave me.

A few hours later I made a trip to the infant floor, mainly because of a temporary lull in my own schedule and mild curiosity about the situation. The nurse listened intently to my description of the child and family, then began pulling the cards of patients who might match. Two, three, and finally six cards were picked, all bearing the names of infants under sixteen months of age, who were admitted in the middle of the night. Some had bizarre injuries such as teeth marks; all had inadequate histories to explain their condition. In each case there was question of the family's contribution to the child's injuries. If I had thought in such terms at all, I would have considered the original case unique, but in a few minutes' revealing talk with the nurse, abuse had become a *class* of events, with ramifications far beyond one infant, one family, one admission.

In my experience as a social worker, I had occasionally come across cases of child abuse. An especially gruesome instance concerned the torture of a seven-year-old by one parent while the other pumped the player piano to drown out his screams. I remember the shock and repugnance at hearing this story; such a reaction, I believe, typifies the feelings of most of us toward child abuse. It was only some years later, when abuse emerged as a class of events, that I was able to gain a measure of objectivity toward it. As a class and not a unique occurrence, it took shape as a phenomenon of American society that could be studied and might ultimately be understood. The search for ways of helping the families and their children would of course always come first. In addition were questions of etiology, incidence, family dynamics, professional attitudes, cultural pressures, involvement with the law and with medicine, and many more.

Over the next few years I became convinced that the quality of child care was a crucial factor in the health management of all children, particularly infants and preschoolers. This conviction, however, was not shared by most hospital staff, who thought that ensuring immunizations, proper nutrition, and medical care when necessary were enough to safeguard a child. Personnel of all disciplines were poorly attuned to the grave social problems masked by the presenting injuries of the victimized child. Some physicians concentrated on the physical condition of the patient, shutting out the signs of interpersonal difficulties that might be central to his condition. Others, aware of the implications of the child's injuries, were driven by anger and indignation to accuse the parents, who responded with heightened defensiveness. Social workers too resisted the possibility of abuse or neglect, and, in consequence, did not seek the pertinent facts regarding the family's ability to care for the child.

Like hospital personnel, helping persons in the community were divided between complete denial of the phenomenon and belief that guilty parents should be severely punished. Few individuals were able to muster the composure necessary to look at the families with an open mind and a measure of compassion. Little ongoing counseling was available for abusive parents and there were few protective resources for their wounded children. Court dispositions were unpredictable and evinced a lack of suitable guidelines. Even when an especially outrageous case finally came before the court, a lack of understanding was apparent. At this early time in the development of knowledge about abuse, the newspapers carried the story of an infant with multiple injuries so extensive that the attending physician likened them to those which might be sustained through a fall from a three-story building. The parents, in court on charges of inflicting the trauma, were acquitted because the jury believed their story that the baby had injured himself playing with a plastic rattle.

Throughout the nation there existed the same dearth of understanding or interest. Important questions existed, but answers were sparse. What were the clues to child abuse? Nobody knew. What systematic hospital procedures were invoked when abuse was suspected? None. Who worked with the parents? Medical personnel appropriate to the child's physical condition but not individuals trained to assess behavior, such as psychologists, social workers, and psychiatrists. What provisions were made for the child's safety following discharge? None, beyond ensuring that the physical condition would be watched. If the parent brought the child to the hospital, then the parent took the child home, with no questions asked, except in the most blatant of cases. When I sought answers to these questions, I found no helpful information in medical or social work journals until the United States Children's Bureau referred me to a state journal which discussed how parental abuse had caused orthopedic problems in some young children.

The time thus seemed ripe for a study of abused children and their families. In 1958, I began the study that was to appear in 1967 as *Children in Jeopardy*. In casting about for suitable subjects, I learned that the chief of radiology at Children's Hospital and a pediatric colleague had painstakingly reviewed the x-ray films for all the children seen in the department for the previous thirteen years and had culled the films of fifty children with roentgen evidence of multiple skeletal injuries, that is, several fractures in various stages of healing, implying a series of traumatic incidents. One fracture may be the result of an accident, but it is hard to imagine that a well-cared-for child would have a series of accidents resulting in fractures.

The physicians who selected these films designated the children as abused and arranged with me to study them. But before any attempt was made to see parents or children, I engaged the help of student assistants, and we spent many months reading the available records on the families. These included the Children's Hospital records and material from the Juvenile Court and the County Board of Assistance. Ultimately, when we felt we had digested the agency data, plans were made to approach the families and begin evaluation of the children. Funding was provided by the National Institute of Mental Health; I was the director of the project and the co-directors were the radiologist, the pediatrician, and the head of the psychiatric department, each of whom participated in specific parts of the children's evaluations. As all the staff met regularly to assess the data for each family, this may have been the first time that a team was utilized in the investigation of child abuse.

But, unknown to me at that time, there had been earlier stirrings of awareness. In 1946, John Caffey had published an article linking subdural hematomas and fractures of the long bones in infants. The article did not specifically implicate parents, although Caffey was aware of their possible involvement, for he had found tremendous resistance to the idea on the part of medical colleagues. He presented six well-documented cases of traumatized infants, raised and refuted the possibility of disease as the cause of the injuries, and left open the question of etiology. Caffey's article is generally credited with being the pioneer publication in relation to the abused infant. However, this article and other early ones were either published in journals I would never have thought of consulting or bore medical titles that gave no clue to any connection with abuse.

A long dry period with no reports on the subject was broken by the publication of a report from Silverman (1953), a former student of Caffey, who termed physical trauma "probably the most common disease of infancy." He noted the resistance of physicians to the possibility that parental mistreatment could account for the serious injuries of children, and he deplored the search for obscure disease syndromes to account for the fractures. The next dry period was shorter. In 1955, Woolley and Evans published findings concerning twelve families of children with suspicious injuries. A high incidence of neurotic or psychotic behavior was found among the parents.

Reports then began appearing more frequently, and sentiment to "do something" grew. Probably the greatest pressure was generated by the work of Kempe and his associates in Colorado. With a fortunate felicity, Kempe invented the term "the battered child" (Kempe, Silverman, Steele, Droegemueller, and Silver, 1962), a phrase that "brought it all together" and marshaled many disparate forces to promote professional and community awareness and to insert new provisions into the law for the protection of mistreated children.

As we were completing the study eventually published as *Children in Jeopardy*, we became aware of the overlap between infant accident and abuse and the difficulty in distinguishing between the two. We received funding in 1964 to study a group of infants referred to the hospital because of a traumatic incident with the aim of describing the characteristics of abusive and nonabusive families and their children. We began to see the children and families in 1966 and completed the study in 1968. The intent was to do a follow-up and this was accomplished in 1974, when the children were between eight and ten years old. The present book describes these two studies.

The role of physicians such as Caffey, Silverman, Woolley, Evans, and Kempe in bringing child abuse into professional and public awareness is noteworthy. Social work has traditionally been charged with the protection of ill-treated children and the rehabilitation of their families. Although this task had been carried out for many years, child protection remained predominantly a case-centered activity until a few physicians became alerted to the problem. Progress toward a comprehensive formulation of child abuse is, of course, the result of the efforts of many individuals from diverse backgrounds. Various cultural changes have also contributed. But an essential spur was the diagnostic acumen, compassion, and professional influence of some of the medical community.

In the early 1960s, the Children's Bureau called a special meeting of concerned professionals to consider whether official recognition should be made of this phenomenon, child abuse, and what form the recognition should take. I had the good fortune to be present both at this initial meeting and at the second one, held several months later. As would be true for some years, there was strong feeling that abuse was an infrequent though important occurrence. The concern was voiced that official recognition would have the drawback of concentrating too much attention on a small, bizarre element of child care. Another underlying feeling (at least according to my perception) was reluctance to arouse the strong emotions that would undoubtedly result from official recognition. But finally the decision was taken to formulate a model child-abuse reporting law for consideration by the states.

It is a matter of common knowledge that the states, without exception, embraced the concept of reporting mistreated children to an official agency: by 1967 all the states had their own laws, most of which were mandatory. Unfortunately, since the majority of states provided no funds for the additional personnel that would be required for reasonable implementation, the legislation was often no more than a pious expression of worthy sentiment.

Once the state laws were passed, interest in child abuse waned for a time. Few new investigations could be funded and reports in the literature, though not sparse, were far from voluminous. Activities behind the scenes, however, were vigorous, and resulted, in 1974, in the passage of PL 93-247, the federal legislation that created the National Center of Child Abuse and Neglect. Interestingly, the federal government opposed this move on the basis that ample funding was available from already established sources for continued work on the problem.

The results of the 1974 legislation can be seen on every side: demonstration projects, research, self-help groups, evaluation of treatment modalities. With justification, many professionals complain of the lack of an overall plan, for results are not cumulative and no long-range goals have been spelled out. Nevertheless, the current situation is very different from twenty years ago. For example, in some hospitals parents now must screw up their courage to bring a child with any kind of traumatic injury. The parents may be separated from their offspring while the child is subjected to an interrogation designed to make him implicate one or both of the parents as the aggressor who caused the injury.

But the present professional attitudes toward abuse, extreme though they may sometimes be, are allowing some light to come through. As a whole, the professional community is empathetic toward parents, aware of their problems, and interested in helping. Child abuse is no longer a taboo term. The search now must be for ways of preventing abuse, for helping parents find better ways of socializing their offspring.

Acknowledgments

The study that resulted in this book is a product of the collaborative efforts of many individuals and their organizations. My co-investigators Sue Evans, M.S.W., and John B. Reinhart, M.D., are both of Children's Hospital of Pittsburgh. The four interviewers who conducted the home interviews and, at the conclusion of the study, relayed the recommendations of the study staff to each of the mothers were Francine Carter, Herman Jones, Randy Miller, and Carol Sankey. Rick Alexander, Coordinator, had the difficult job of finding the comparison children and obtaining their parents' consent to enter the follow-up study.

The eight clinical examiners who conducted the evaluations of the children were stimulating to work with because of their investment in the study and the ideas they contributed. They were:

Lawrence Bloom, Ph.D., Director of the Speech Clinic, Children's Hospital of Pittsburgh

Lenore Farmer, M.D., Pediatrician, Western Psychiatric Institute and Clinic, School of Medicine, University of Pittsburgh

F. Gordon Foster, M.D., Assistant Professor of Psychiatry, Western Psychiatric Institute and Clinic, School of Medicine, University of Pittsburgh

Eleanor C. Irwin, Ph.D., Expressive Arts Therapist and Clinical Assistant Professor of Child Psychiatry, Pittsburgh Child Guidance Center

Elaine Malloy, M.S.W., Expressive Arts Therapist, Western Psychiatric Institute and Clinic, School of Medicine, University of Pittsburgh

Richard McPartland, Principal Research Assistant, Western Psychiatric Institute and Clinic, School of Medicine, University of Pittsburgh

Michael Sherlock, M.D., Pediatrician, Children's Hospital of Pittsburgh

Alan Strange, Psychologist, Indiana University of Pennsylvania

Carol Sankey was a valued research assistant and literary critic. Kathy Lee prepared the original report. Gloria Miner, Administrative Assistant, made the wheels turn and also gave generously of her skills. Both Gloria and Kathy made themselves available whenever and wherever they were needed. Abby Levine provided editorial assistance in the preparation of the manuscript for publication. Not only did she proffer needed advice concerning style and organization; she also raised substantive questions which were provocative and helpful.

Four organizations gave support to the project. These were Children's Hospital of Pittsburgh, Western Psychiatric Institute and Clinic, the University of Pittsburgh Graduate School of Public Health, and Pittsburgh Child Guidance Center; the backing of all was essential to the completion of the work. We are also indebted to the Child Welfare Services of Allegheny County, Fayette County, and Beaver County, Pennsylvania, all of whom were generous in sharing essential data with the staff.

We are grateful for the financial support contributed to the project from the following sources:

Health Services Improvement Branch
Division of Clinical Services
Bureau of Community Health Services
Department of Health, Education and Welfare
Washington, D.C.

The Maurice Falk Medical Fund
Pittsburgh, Pennsylvania

The University of Pittsburgh Medical Alumni Association

Introduction

Although child abuse is a subject of much concern in this country, there has been little study of the development of abused children after their mistreatment. In this study, which defines abuse as physical assault or excessive physical punishment directed against a child regardless of whether injury was inflicted, the long-range goal is to study a sample of abused children at intervals until they are adults with their own children. The immediate goal, the basis of this book, is to compare seventeen abused children with seventeen who had suffered accidents, eight years after all were examined in the Infant Accident Study, a descriptive study of one-hundred families and their one-hundred-and-one children that began in 1964.[1] The thirty-four children examined in the follow-up study were matched on age, race, sex, and socioeconomic status; other than the provision of substitute care for some abused children, there had been no individualized treatment of either parents or children. A second comparison group, matched on the same variables, consisted of children with no recorded history of abuse and no reported accidents resulting in hospital treatment before the age of one year. These children were not part of the Infant Accident Study; they were selected and studied only in the follow-up investigation. We must emphasize that this is not a study of child abuse across-the-board, but a comparison of certain abused children with nonabused children, taking into account social class, among other variables. Since social class was predominantly low, we have no opportunity to talk about abuse in higher social classes.

Data are available from three periods in the lives of the traumatized children. (The term *traumatized* will be used throughout to refer to children who suffered either abuse or accidents.) Chapter 1 describes the Infant Accident Study, in which Time One (T_1) refers to the time of the family's inclusion in the study, and Time Two (T_2) to the period one year later when the final evaluation was completed. Results of the Infant Accident Study are presented in the form of a reanalysis of the early family and child data for the thirty-four children who were also the subjects of the follow-up study eight years later. Data for the families are more limited than for the children because a child protection agency removed several abused children from their own homes between Time One and Time Two and placed them in substitute homes. As a matter of policy, we decided not to continue interviewing parents no longer caring for their children. No purpose would have been served in opening a subject that might be painful.

In chapter 2, we describe the follow-up study, Time Three (T_3). Findings are presented for the thirty-four children and their present caretakers. Data for the untraumatized children of the comparison group are given for Time Three, the only period in which this group was studied. Chapter 3 presents case studies of three of the children and their families. The book concludes with a discussion of the implications of this investigation for future social policy.

Thirty-four children is of course a small sample. Pennsylvania had no mandatory reporting law in 1964, the year when the Infant Accident Study was first funded. Thus, it was not possible to identify a large number of children officially reported as abused. The significance of this study lies in its prospective nature and in the fact that abused children were compared with two carefully matched comparison groups: children who had sustained infantile accidents and children with no record of abuse or early accidents.

A few previous studies have focused on the long-range outcome of child abuse (Elmer, 1967; Silver, Dublin, and Lourie, 1969; Morse, Sahler, and Friedman, 1970; Martin, Beezley, Conway, and Kempe, 1974). The results were in general agreement that many of these unfortunate children turn out to be intellectually retarded and develop social and emotional problems. A serious drawback in each study, however, was the absence of a comparison group matched on relevant demographic variables. Child abuse is known to be intertwined with a number of other negative conditions such as prematurity, failure-to-thrive, lack of environmental stimulation, and poor parent-child relationships. When social class, age, sex, and race are additional confounding variables, the findings must be interpreted with caution.

The use of scientifically chosen comparison groups should help correct conclusions based on the study of abused children alone. Follow-up data that are as valid as possible should help direct efforts to protect children and support their parents.

FRAGILE FAMILIES, TROUBLED CHILDREN

CHAPTER 1

The Infant Accident Study

This study was designed to identify possible physical, developmental, and behavioral differences between abused and nonabused infants seen in the radiology department of Children's Hospital of Pittsburgh. Additional aims were to evaluate and categorize the families of the infants and ascertain the differences between families with deviant child care practices and those practicing adequate child care. The criteria for selection of the infants were (1) an age of twelve months or less; (2) referral to the radiology department because of suspected abuse or an impact accident (that is, a fall or blow; other types of accidents such as ingestions or burns were excluded); and (3) residence with the natural family within the four-county area comprising the Greater Pittsburgh Standard Metropolitan Statistical Area. Disease could not be a factor in the diagnosis.

We began with a daily review of the x-ray requisitions for babies of eligible age and residence. When the pediatrician found no evidence of disease, we immediately sought the participation of the mother and made an appointment for a home interview by a social worker. The semi-structured interview covered demographic information, the circumstances of the injury, the family's reaction to the traumatic incident, and the mother's perception of family stress since conception of the index child (a term which will be used throughout this book to designate the child under study). It was often difficult to acquire subjects because parents suspected the study was designed to prove abuse and remove the infants from their homes. The families of children who had suffered accidents felt as guilty and suspicious as abusive parents, probably because accidents to infants are commonly perceived as the fault of the caretakers. Despite this initial resistance, after one or two contacts the majority of nonabusive mothers were able to enter into a positive relationship with the interviewer and ultimately with the rest of the research staff. This was in contrast with some abusive mothers, who rarely refused to make an appointment but simply were not there at the time agreed upon. The interviewer, an experienced social worker, was tireless in her efforts to engage them, but in some cases no amount of effort was enough.

After the home interview, the mother was asked to bring the child to the outpatient department of the hospital, where the Infant Accident Study pediatrician took a health history and examined the child. If the child was too ill, the outpatient examination was deferred until his or her recovery. The same pediatrician conducted all the assessments, which included a developmental evaluation and an assessment of behavioral characteristics. The mother was asked for information concerning pregnancy, labor, delivery, and the neonatal period, and this was also gathered through hospital records. We had planned to interview fathers too, as we had observed their frequent involvement in child care. Several fathers were seen, but scheduling difficulties and the unavailability of many men through separation, divorce, or desertion vitiated the effort for any systematic research purpose.

After the home visit and the hospital outpatient session, a judgment was made by the director of the Infant Accident Study, the social work interviewer, and the pediatrician as to the cause of the child's referral to the radiology department. The child was classified as abused if one or more of the following conditions were present: (1) admission of abuse by a parent or report of abuse of the patient or a sibling; (2) an inadequate or contradictory explanation of the child's condition; or (3) more than one injury, incurred at different times. A child could not be classified as abused unless all the judges agreed. All other children were termed *accident* children. We did not differentiate among the criteria as to potency, but judged a child abused if any one of the three conditions was applicable. With respect to the majority of children classified as abused, one of the criteria was satisfied, usually report of abuse. Several children were eligible on the basis of two of the criteria, and a few others on the basis of all three.

An initial identification of abuse usually requires some degree of inference because caretakers do not readily admit to assaulting a child. By Time Two, however, the end of the year of study, a substantial body of additional information had been gained about the caretakers and their habitual child care practices, through a second home visit, observation of a feeding at home, a questionnaire mailed to the family, a final outpatient evaluation of the baby, and a second assessment of behavioral characteristics. At this time the original judgments concerning abuse and accident were reviewed and, where necessary, altered in the light of the parental reports and staff observations. We determined whether later information had confirmed or negated the original judgment of abuse or accident and added a new criterion for abuse, direct evidence. This consisted of observation, a mother's report, or physical signs of assault or excessive punishment directed at the index child or a sibling. Thus, the Time One assessment of abuse or accident was confined to judging the nature of a single incident, the one that had brought the child and his family to the attention of the Infant Accident Study. The Time Two assessment was broader in that we considered not only the initial incident but also evidence of undue physical force in the family's customary handling of the child.

In the course of reassessment we found that certain families who could not be judged abusive were nevertheless providing deficient care. Five types of deficiency could be perceived: (1) failure to protect the child from serious environmental dangers; (2) failure to provide essential medical care despite repeated careful explanation; (3) failure to provide a competent caretaker for prolonged periods of parental absence; (4) encouragement of the baby to participate in motor activities far beyond his or her ability; and (5) failure to provide minimum daily care. The presence of one or more of these deficiencies led to an additional classification of neglect. A family could be judged both abusive and neglectful, lose an original abuse rating, or acquire one. To lose an abuse rating did not signify that the family was once abusive and then recovered, but that the initial rating was considered erroneous. Conversely, a family might acquire an abuse rating not because its members suddenly became violent, but because of our increased knowledge about them. (Abusive behavior toward a child may indeed fluctuate over time, but the staff was not trying to identify such cycles; our goal was to judge accurately which families were prone to overt abusive behavior.)

Out of the one hundred families observed in the Infant Accident Study twenty-six were judged abusive at Time One. Nineteen of these were also judged abusive at Time Two; in addition, fifteen of the nineteen acquired a judgment of neglect at that time. Five of the families termed accident at Time One were recategorized as abusive at Time Two. The nineteen families judged abusive at both Time One and Time Two were termed *high certainty*; the five judged abusive at Time Two but not Time One were termed *lower certainty*. Because we were unable to find matching accident children for all nineteen high-certainty children, the final sample of seventeen abused children chosen for the follow-up study was selected from the high-certainty and lower-certainty groups: twelve of these were high-certainty and five were lower-certainty abused children. Thus, none of the children chosen for the follow-up study were judged abused only at Time One; they were considered abused either at both times or at Time Two only. Eight of the twelve high-certainty children were considered neglected as well as abused. The stigmata of neglect are one of the major factors in the early recognition of abuse among infants because the infantile response to severe neglect is relatively immediate and also highly visible in terms of weight loss, apathy, and/or developmental retardation. In the absence of injury, it is considerably more difficult to diagnose abuse in the well-developed and well-nourished infant, especially if the family is fairly presentable and verbal. This was the situation with respect to the five lower-certainty children, all of whom appeared adequately cared for upon entering the Infant Accident Study. Observations over the period of the study, however, demonstrated the harsh and unusual nature of the physical punishment employed by the parents, primarily the mother.

The seventeen accident children were drawn from a pool of sixty-three children who were judged accident at both Time One and Time Two. Throughout our description of the reanalysis of the Infant Accident Study, comparisons are made between the entire abuse group and the entire accident group; between the high-certainty and lower-certainty abuse subgroups; and between the high-certainty abuse subgroup and its matching subgroup of accident children.[1] (The technique for matching is described in the discussion of the follow-up study.)

The Families

The seventeen abusive and seventeen accident families were compared at Time One on the basis of demographic characteristics. Throughout the one-year study, we gathered data on the variables of stability, support, and maternal behavior toward the child as shown in physical child care, attitudes toward punishment, expectations concerning infant behavior, and perception of the child. We hypothesized that abusive families are subject to more stress of all types than nonabusive families and that they have fewer emotional supports, such as members of the extended family, friends, or community groups. We also anticipated that they would provide poorer physical care, would punish more harshly, and would have higher expectations and more negative perceptions of their offspring.

Demographic characteristics. The two groups were compared on the basis of the mother's age, race, marital status, living status (with husband, boyfriend, relatives, friends, or alone), and education; on the income per household member; and on the family's socioeconomic status. The last was assessed according to the Hollingshead Two-Factor Index of Social Position (1957), which classifies socioeconomic status into five categories ranging from I (highest) to V (lowest) on the basis of education and occupation.

Stability. Abusive families have been described as dependent and immature and "living with a very precarious sense of stability" (Pollock and Steele, 1972). Our index of stability was based on characteristics contributing to independence, resiliency, familial permanence, and comparative freedom from stress, and consisted of seven items:

1. The mother's living status. Studies over the last quarter century have shown the importance of a male partner to the family (Hill, 1949), the stressful effects of the loss of a spouse (Holmes and Rahe, 1967), the particular harm to an abusive parent caused by loss or alienation of a partner (Pollock and Steele, 1972), and the negative effect of absence of a father on child development (Herzog and Sudia, 1973).

2. Adequacy of income.[2]

3. Source of income (that is, from a job or other private source, as opposed to welfare).

4. Number of family moves. Frequent moves are a contemporary American phenomenon, and changes in schools, disruptions of friendships, and difficulties in establishing bonds in a new community can all affect families and children adversely. High geographic mobility has been seen as a component of family instability (Martin et al., 1974).

5. The mother's health. Her energy and sense of well being can help maintain family equilibrium, while poor maternal health may weaken her capacity to care for children and help the family cope with changing circumstances.[3] Among the problems that Baldwin and Oliver (1975) found in abusive families were "excesses of psychiatric and physical illness and disability."

6. Amount of family stress.[4] Whatever the nature of the pressures affecting the family, the final effects are seen in interpersonal relations. We have defined stress as any event, acute or chronic, that creates anxiety in the individual, produces disruption in the family organization by adding or removing a member, or causes emotional or physical difficulty for a member. Because stressful events create tension and require psychological adjustment, we believed that they might increase the difficulty of caring for chil-

dren. Several investigators have defined family stress as a major factor contributing to child abuse (Elmer, 1967; Ebbin, Gollub, Stein, and Wilson, 1969; Gil, 1970; Justice and Duncan, 1976). Pollock and Steele (1972) have pointed out the relatively trivial nature of some events perceived by abusive parents as crises, such as the breaking down of a washing machine. We hypothesized that the abusive mothers perceived a greater amount of stress in the months preceding the traumatic incident than did the accident mothers.

7. Continuity of the family's care of the index child. Whether voluntary or not, placement of a child away from home for one or more prolonged periods detracts from the sense of permanence of both child and family.

A list of these items and their scoring is included in Appendix 1a. Each of the seven items was analyzed separately and their scores were combined to yield an overall stability rating. The higher the score, the more stable the family was considered.

Support. It is generally agreed that abusive individuals lack a supportive environment. They have been described as isolated (Schneider, Pollock, and Helfer, 1972), almost devoid of associations outside the home (Elmer, 1967), and without social support (Newberger and Hyde, 1975).[5] Despite the wide recognition of the importance of support, few attempts have been made to specify and measure its components.

For the follow-up study, we developed an index of possible sources of support and modified it slightly to analyze the Time One–Time Two data. It consisted of six items, of which all but the third were pre-coded:

1. Availability of another person to confide in. The therapeutic value of "talking it out" has long been recognized in psychiatry and other helping fields as well as by the Roman Catholic Church. Confiding in another person can also substitute for the physical expression of aggressive feelings.

2. Availability of a male partner. This item is related to the first item on the stability scale but differs in that it does not require living together. An available male is seen as an important part of a

support system for a mother, just as his presence would contribute to familial stability.

3. Expressed dissatisfaction with the male partner. Although a male might be on the scene infrequently or erratically, the mother would receive more support than if there were no male partner at all. However, conflict with the partner would dilute the strength of the support the mother felt. Items two and three together permitted a wider range of combined scores, thus reflecting the situation more accurately.[6]

4. Availability of help from friends or neighbors. The mother would receive support from knowing there were at least one or two people from whom she could confidently expect assistance if she requested it.

5. The importance of religion. Religion was seen as a source of both spiritual solace and social support, through association with others in church membership.

6. The use of a regular source of medical care for the child. This was considered a potentially good source of support for mothers of infants and was rated by the pediatrician on the basis of information reported by the mother during the pediatric history.

The support index and scoring system appear in Appendix 1b. As with the stability index, each item was analyzed separately, after which scores for the six items were added for an overall support score.

Mother's behavior in relation to the child. We examined three aspects of child-related maternal behavior:

1. Child care.[7] Infants are completely dependent upon their caretakers and are especially vulnerable to poor care. Studies have shown abusive families to attend to their children's health needs erratically (Holman and Kanwar, 1975). We examined well-child care, sick-child care, immunizations, and overall physical care.

2. Attitudes toward punishment and maternal expectations of the child. Because of the obvious connection between abuse and harsh methods of punishment (Pollock and Steele, 1972), we tried to ascertain how the mother would go about teaching right from wrong, what baby behavior she considered punishable with what

methods, how she would expect to respond if the baby should hit or bite her, and at what age she would expect the baby to know right from wrong. The first three topics were examined as to the mother's use of physical punishment versus other methods. Responses to the fourth item were divided into two groups: mothers who expected knowledge of right and wrong to exist when the child was twelve months or younger, and those who expected it to develop after one year.

3. Perception of the child.[8] Several investigators have found that abusive parents tend to perceive their offspring in a distorted fashion (Galdston, 1965; Greenberg, 1970; Terr, 1970; Baher, Hyman, C. Jones, R. Jones, Kerr, and Mitchell, 1976). Galdston (1971) noted the inconsistencies and exaggerations that characterized these mothers' comments about their children. When a parent sees a baby as overdemanding, bad, or willful, it may not be difficult for him or her to justify harsh measures against the child.

The Families: Findings ✕

As expected, the abusive and accident families showed marked differences in relation to the variables of stability, support, and maternal behavior toward the child.

Demographic characteristics. Tables 1 and 2 show the characteristics of the abusive and accident mothers at Time One. As can be seen, the sample is heavily weighted toward the lower end of the socioeconomic scale (classes IV and V). The abusive mothers were more apt to be unmarried and living alone. They also had somewhat less education and lower monthly income per household member. None of the mothers in either group were working at either Time One or Time Two, and their income thus came either from the Department of Public Assistance or the male partner. Even though many fathers were absent (therefore, no information on them appears in table 1), it was possible to ascertain the occupations of all but three. Most jobs, particularly of men in the abuse group, were in the lower echelons of labor, for example, car washer or laundry worker. Men in the accident-group families tended to

TABLE 1. Demographic Characteristics

	Age		Race		Marital Status		Living Status	
	Mean (Yrs.)	Range (Yrs.)	Black	White	Married	Other[a]	With Someone[b]	Alone
Abuse (n=17)	24.18	19–39	9	8	8	9	11	6
Accident (n=17)	24.76	18–33	9	8	11	6	15	2

a. "Other" includes single, separated, divorced, or widowed.
b. "With Someone" includes living with husband, boyfriend, relatives, or friends.
c. The education of the abusive mothers was significantly lower than that of the accident mothers: $t_{32} = 2.19$, $p < .05$. No other statistical tests related to table 1 were significant.

TABLE 2. Demographic Characteristics

	Age		Race		Marital Status		Living Status	
	Mean (Yrs.)	Range (Yrs.)	White	Black	Married	Other[a]	With Someone[b]	Alone
High certainty (n=12)	23.4	19–39	4	8	3	9	6	6
Lower certainty (n=5)	26.0	21–35	4	1	5	0	5	0

	Race	Marital Status	Living Status
Test	Fisher's Exact Prob., 2-tailed	Fisher's Exact Prob., 2-tailed	Fisher's Exact Prob., 2-tailed
Level of significance	N.S.	$p = .02$	N.S.

a. "Other" includes single, separated, divorced, or widowed.
b. "With Someone" includes living with husband, boyfriend, relatives, or friends.

of the Abusive and Accident Mothers, Time One (T_1)

Education[c]		Income per Month (Per Person)		Socioeconomic Status				
< High School	≥ High School	Mean	Range	I	II	III	IV	V
10	7	$85.40	$25–$167	0	1	1	5	10
5	12	$102.00	$23–$233	0	1	2	4	10

of the High- and Lower-Certainty Abusive Mothers, T_1

Education		Income per Month (Per Person)		Socioeconomic Status				
< High School	≥ High School	Mean	Range	I	II	III	IV	V
10	2	$88.27	$25–$167	0	0	0	3	9
0	5	$95.33	$30–$167	0	1	1	2	1

Education	Income per Month (Per Person)		SES
$t_{15} = 2.93$			$\chi^2 = 6.89$ df $= 2$
$p = .02$	N.S.		$p \leqslant .05$

have jobs with more status and higher pay, such as phone installer and teacher. Less education and poorer jobs among abusive parents have also been reported by Gil (1970). Statistically significant differences appeared between the high-certainty and lower-certainty subgroups of the abuse sample (see table 2 for statistics on the mothers). Compared with the lower-certainty subgroup, the high-certainty subgroup was disadvantaged as to education, marital status, and socioeconomic class.

Stability.   The mean score for abusive mothers was 7.06, range 0–13; the mean for the accident mothers was 10.06, range 5–14. The highest possible score was 14, which indicated excellent stability as judged by this instrument. Total scores showed significant differences for each group comparison: (1) abuse versus accident; (2) high certainty versus lower; and (3) high certainty versus their matched accidents. In the first comparison, the abusive mothers scored significantly lower as to total stability ($t_{32} = 2.06$, $p<.05$) and maternal health ($x^2 = 11.91$, $p < .01$) and significantly higher in amount of stress ($x^2 = 8.19$, $p < .05$). In the second, the high-certainty mothers scored significantly lower than the lower certainty in total stability ($t_{15} = 2.91$, $p<.05$), although there were no significant differences as to maternal health and amount of stress. The high-certainty mothers scored significantly lower than their matched accidents on the first two of these variables ($t_{22} = 3.06$, $p<.01$; Fisher's Exact Probability, $p = .05$) and higher on amount of stress ($x^2 = 6.60$, $p < .05$). For the variables of living status, adequacy of income, number of family moves, and continuity of child care, there were no significant group differences, but there was a tendency for the abuse group to score lower than the accident. No significant differences were found between the groups as to private source of income.

The abusive mothers scored lower than the accident on each individual item of the stability index. However, only stress and maternal health differentiated the groups at a significant level. Six of the abusive but none of the accident mothers perceived the greatest possible amount of stress according to our scoring system. We also found a difference between the two groups in the number of individual mothers who reported specific types of stress (table 3). This was especially striking with respect to accidents and physical assaults. One abusive mother, for example, said she had been raped by three men during daylight hours while she was en route to the hospital with her child; she called this an accident. The credibility of this report is questionable, but it resembled the reports of other abusive mothers in its focus on violence, whether real or fantasied.

TABLE 3. Rank Order of Stress Events According to the Number of Abusive and Accident Mothers Reporting Each Event, T_1

	Abusive (n = 17)		Accident (n = 17)	
Rank	Type of Event	Number of Mothers Reporting	Type of Event	Number of Mothers Reporting
1	Moves	8	Physical illness	7
2	Accidents and physical assaults	7	Moves Death Other separations	3 3 3
3	Physical illness Pregnancy and delivery (index child)	5 5	Emotional illness Divorce/separation Additions to family	2 2 2
4	Institutionalization Other separations	4 4	Pregnancy and delivery (index child) Alcoholism Accidents and physical assaults	1 1 1

Five abusive mothers but only one accident mother saw the pregnancy with the index baby as stressful. This is even more interesting when compared with the objective medical data: the number of women with physical difficulties associated with pregnancy for the index child was approximately the same for the two groups. Conventional wisdom has it that the pains and tribulations of carrying and giving birth to a baby recede quickly into forgetfulness. Our finding suggests that for abusive women such memories remain comparatively fresh. Theoretically, this could hamper the formation of a nurturing relationship with the baby.

The other item on the stability index that distinguished abusive from accident mothers was health. More abusive than accident mothers had multiple health problems. For example, one abusive mother, Mrs. A., suffered from mental retardation, depression, chronic medical problems, and obesity. Among Mrs. A.'s medical problems was a significant heart condition that had been recommended for surgery when she was fourteen years old. Not only had she avoided the operation; she had never returned to the physician who had examined her. When we saw her at the age of twenty-eight, Mrs. A. had chronic arthritis affecting her legs and arms and had recently put her hand through a window, severing a tendon. Her capacity to judge the need for medical attention was diminished by her retardation, and she also found it difficult to exert any effort such as would be required to get herself to a medical resource.

There was almost no difference between the two groups regarding the number of individual mothers who had chronic medical problems: five abusive and four accident mothers. Taken together, these nine mothers represent more than 25 percent of the total Time One–Time Two sample. We had not anticipated that so high a proportion of relatively young women should be subject to so many handicapping conditions. Besides arthritis, the conditions included high blood pressure, diabetes, renal disease, and anemia.

Support. Total support scores showed significant differences for abuse versus accident ($t_{27} = 2.45$, $p < .05$) and for the high-certainty subgroup versus its matched accident subgroup ($t_{18} = 2.69$, $p < .05$). The mean score for the abuse group was 7.44 and for the accident group 9.31, compared with a possible high score of 11.[9] We were surprised to find that the mothers in the abuse group were more involved with religious activities, attending services more frequently than did those in the accident group. For all other items the abusive mothers had lower scores, but these were significant only for dissatisfaction with the male (abuse less satisfied than accident, $x^2 = 4.02$, $p < .05$) and for regular medical care (high certainty less than matched accidents, Fisher's Exact Probability, $p = .05$). Nevertheless, the results were in accordance with our original hypotheses, as shown by the overall comparisons.

There has been much more effort devoted to the study of stress than to the study of support, although the two variables appear closely related. The perception of stress is idiosyncratic and may vary independently of objective facts: loss of the father's job is perceived as less devastating if there are grandparents who can help. In the same manner (though less dramatically), the perception of support may vary independently of the facts. For example, a mother may view her parents as nonsupportive even though they would be more than willing to help; or she may think of a friend as a dependable support whereas the friend would drop out at the first sign of trouble. The balance between perceived stress and perceived support is the crucial measure: when one has a feeling of support, apparently the sense of stress is lower, and vice versa.

Since the abusive mothers had lower scores in both stability and support, a Pearson product-moment correlation was run between the two sets of scores. This proved to be .62. The association seems logical since the existence of good support should contribute to family stability.

Mother's behavior in relation to the child.   The following results were established from studying the three aspects of this variable:

1. Child care. There were no significant differences in well-child care between any of the groups that were compared. The same was true of immunizations at Time One except that the high-certainty mothers were less prone to ensure immunizations at the correct time. The sick-child care provided by the abusive group proved inferior to that offered by the accident group ($x^2 = 6.30$, $p < .05$). A significant difference also appeared between the high-certainty subgroup and its matched accident subgroup ($x^2 = 7.67$, $p < .05$). No differences were shown in physical child care except that the high-certainty subgroup exhibited poorer care than the lower-certainty subgroup, but not at a significant level. When the four items (well-child care, sick-child care, immunizations, and physical

care) were added to make a child care index for Time One, the following significant differences appeared:

Abuse versus accident: $t_{27} = 2.77$, $p < .01$
High certainty versus lower certainty: $t_{12} = 2.80$, $p < .01$
High certainty versus matched accident: $t_{17} = 3.45$, $p < .01$

In each comparison, the group mentioned first had the lower rating.

2. Attitudes toward punishment and maternal expectations of the child. Although answers to the four questions about punishment and maternal expectations revealed few differences among the major groups, we did learn that knowledge about child development was woefully lacking in the entire sample of mothers. Many thought that children should know right from wrong at the age of four or five months and one mother thought a baby was born knowing this. When asked what they would do if the baby hit, bit, or spit at the mother, most women in both groups indignantly replied they would of course hit back, "to teach the baby he must not do that."

Significant differences appeared between the high-certainty subgroup and its matched accident subgroup as to expectations of when the baby would learn right from wrong. An unexpected finding was that the mothers in the high-certainty subgroup had more realistic expectations (baby would learn when he or she was more than one year old) than their matched accident mothers (Fisher's Exact Probability, $p = .02$), who believed the baby could make moral distinctions when less than one year old. However, the high-certainty mothers were significantly more prepared to use physical punishment to teach the child right from wrong (Fisher's Exact Probability, $p < .05$).

3. Perception of the child. Although a number of aspects of perception were explored (for example, physical appearance, mood, habits), we found no differences in perception between the groups. The majority of mothers were overwhelmingly positive, although in some cases their behavior toward their babies did not correspond to their responses on this variable. We pondered whether

the abusive mothers were covering their true feelings or were genuinely ambivalent and exaggerating the positive. A few mothers did offer spontaneous remarks that were at odds with their seemingly overall positive perception. One called her eighteen-month-old child "a little Communist"; another said her son was "out to get her." Several described their infants as "very good" because they made no demands and were content during the day to lie in a crib in a darkened room while the mothers watched television.

Although we had no hypothesis concerning the mothers' concepts of the ideal parent, in one interview we asked them to describe the ideal mother and father. Without exception, every mother mentioned keeping the baby clean, giving the child material things, or, oddly, being a "proper woman." Many women described the ideal mother in negative terms, as someone who did not run around or sit at bars. The abusive mothers most often described the ideal father in terms of discipline or financial support, and several women said the ideal father should not beat the mother.

The Children

The abused and accident children were assessed as to demographic characteristics, health, mental and motor development, behavioral characteristics, and the number of accidents they incurred between Time One and Time Two. Except for the collection of demographic information and pregnancy and birth records, all data for the children were collected at both Time One and Time Two. We hypothesized that the abused babies would be inferior to the nonabused in health, physical and motor development, acquisition of language, and development of cognitive skills. We anticipated that the abused children would be more irritable and negative but formulated no hypotheses concerning other behavior variables. Three groups of babies were compared: abused versus accident, high-certainty abused versus lower-certainty abused, and high-certainty abused versus its matched accident subgroup.

Demographic characteristics.   At Time One the relevant characteristics were age, race, sex, number of children in the family, and birth order.

Health.   Health data were gathered from the pediatric history given by the mother and the examination of the child. The pediatric history covered pregnancy, labor, birth, the neonatal period, and the baby's subsequent health history. Hospital records concerning pregnancy and birth were used to verify information and provide further details. When the mother's report differed from the records, hospital material was assumed to be more accurate. For example, one mother reported a normal pregnancy and a full-term baby of normal weight, whereas hospital records showed a difficult pregnancy and a premature baby weighing less than five pounds. Perinatal stress was assessed according to the system developed by Werner, Simonian, Bierman, and French (1967). This system addresses all the possible complications of pregnancy, labor, delivery, and the neonatal period as they may apply to either the mother or the infant. Pregnancy and birth history allowed us to estimate the degree to which the newborn might have represented a stress to the mother because of the presence of one or more of these conditions: illegitimate conception or birth, low birth weight, congenital handicaps, birth injuries, poor neonatal health, and high perinatal stress scores. With this information, we could trace the baby's health status from birth through Time Two.

The pediatric examination of the child included systems review, gross neurological screening, and anthropometric measures that were later converted into percentiles for age and sex according to the standard anthropometric growth chart (Stuart and Stevenson, 1950). Percentiles were calculated as closely as possible to provide a range of data for the small number of children. The pediatric examination also allowed us to assess the extent of the injuries, if any, that resulted from the traumatic incident.

Developmental evaluation.   Mental and motor characteristics were evaluated during the pediatric session with the cooperation of the mother. The examiner was a highly experienced pediatrician with special training in the use of developmental instruments. The children were scored on the Cattell Infant Intelligence Scale (1960) and on the research version of the Bayley Scales of Infant Development until the standardization was published (1969). Only the mental and motor scales of the Bayley were utilized.[10]

Behavioral characteristics. We used our own adaptation of the methods developed by Thomas, Chess, Birch, Hertzig, and Korn (1963) to assess mood, activity, and distractibility. The pediatric examination was divided into eight standardized parts during which a specially trained observer tallied baby behavior associated with these three characteristics. We composed a standard form which listed the specific behaviors related to each of the characteristics. For example, smiles or laughs were scored as positive mood, while crying or fussing was tallied as negative mood.[11]

Accidents. Accidents between Time One and Time Two were tracked by periodic inquiries during the interviews, through items on the mailed questionnaire, and by reviewing current entries in the Children's Hospital charts.

The Children: Findings, Time One

Some hypotheses were confirmed while others were not.

Demographic characteristics. Table 4 shows the demographic characteristics of the children when they entered the study. At Time One there was no difference in the number of children per family. This finding is at odds with a report from Light (1973), who found that abusive families with less-educated fathers had more children than nonabusive families with less-educated fathers. The same was true of abusive families with less-educated mothers. Controlling for ethnicity and family income did not affect the results.

There was no group difference as to birth order. Interestingly, all but one of the traumatized children were either the only child or the last of two or more. The exception was an abused twin, considered a middle child because he was the first-born twin. However, because of the age-of-baby criterion ($\leqslant$ twelve months), the subjects in the Infant Accident Study were not likely to have younger siblings.

TABLE 4. Demographic Characteristics of the Children, T_1

| | Age[a] | | White | | Black | | Children in Family | | Birth Order | |
	Mean (Wks.)	Range (Wks.)	Boys	Girls	Boys	Girls	< 3	$\geqslant 3$	1st or Middle	Last
Abuse (n = 17)	32.88	5–55	5	3	7	2	11	6	4	13
Accident (n = 17)	36.93	9–63	5	3	7	2	10	7	7	10

a. One child was 63 weeks old at T_1 because he had been hospitalized for a lengthy period and could not be seen in the outpatient department until this age.

Health. The abuse and accident groups were compared as to birth status, taking into account illegitimate conception or birth, low birth weight, congenital handicaps, birth injuries, neonatal health, and overall perinatal stress scores. Ten of the seventeen abused and eleven of the seventeen accident children had experienced either no problems or only one. The balance of both groups had experienced from two to three problems, with the exception of one abused child whose parents were unmarried and who had a low birth weight, poor neonatal health, and a high perinatal stress score. We were surprised at these findings for two reasons: the even distribution of adverse conditions among both groups and the small number of abused children who exhibited these conditions. This is contrary to previous findings (Klein and Stern, 1971) that health problems at birth are one of the predisposing factors in abuse.

Eleven infants, seven abused and four accident, showed no physical sign of injury when they were brought to the hospital. Four of the seven abused children were referred to the study because of suspicion of abuse, but a skeletal survey by x-ray proved negative. One physical attack that did not result in injury was caused by a mother who admitted trying to smother the child with a pillow but became frightened and instead took the baby to the emergency room. In one of the four uninjured accident cases, an eleven-year-old aunt was carrying the infant boy down steps when she slipped and fell. The baby went over her shoulder and hit his forehead on the wooden steps, but was none the worse except for a nosebleed, which had stopped by the time the family reached the hospital an hour later. Four abused and six accident children had minor injuries such as contusions or soft-tissue swellings. Six abused and seven accident children had serious injuries, for example, intracranial damage, multiple fractures, or combinations of injuries including brain or bone trauma. In summary, slightly more than half of each group (eleven abused and ten accident) sustained either no injury or only mild symptoms as a result of the traumatic incident. The other children suffered comparatively serious physical results.

At Time One we compared the abuse and accident groups as to percentiles for weight, height, and head circumference (table 5).

TABLE 5. Anthropometric Measures for Abused and Accident Children, T_1

	Weight Percentile[a]		Height Percentile		Head Circumference Percentile	
	Mean	Range	Mean	Range	Mean	Range
Abuse (n = 17)	29.8	<3–96	24.5	<3->97	29.7	<3–85
Accident (n = 17)	61.2	<3->97	47.2	<3->97	46.0	<3–55

a. The weight of the accident children was significantly greater than that of the abused children: $t_{32} = 2.73$, $p < .01$. No other statistical results related to table 5 were significant.

On every measure the mean percentile of the abuse group was lower, but only weight showed a significant difference. Comparison of perinatal stress revealed no difference between the major groups.

The number and nature of health problems at Time One are described in table 6. Seven of the abused children but only one accident child had weight below the third percentile for age and sex.[12] This condition, known as *failure-to-thrive*, is frequently found among mistreated infants, even those whose nutrition appears adequate (Koel, 1969; Evans, Reinhart, and Succop, 1972). Three of the seven abused children with weight below the third percentile at Time One had low birth weight; even when this was taken into account, their weights were still below the third percentile. Three of the four children with head injuries also had positive neurological signs. Seven others had positive signs without head injury;[13] six of these were in the abuse group. Other health problems, for example, breath-holding, asthma, and gastroenteritis, were scattered through the whole sample.

All the health problems at Time One (table 6) were totaled for each child and the groups were then compared. Twelve accident

TABLE 6. Health Problems of Abused and Accident Children, T_1

	Low Birth Weight	Neonatal Problems	Congenital Anomalies or Birth Injuries	Weight < 3rd Percentile	Head Injuries	Multiple Skeletal Injuries	Neurological Signs	Other Problems
Abuse (n = 17)	4	4	2	7	3	3	8	7
Accident (n = 17)	0	2	1	1	1	0	2	5

Note: Some of the problems listed in this table pertained to the same children; for example, two of the abused children with low birth weight also had neonatal problems.

children but only two abused children were free from problems. The number of children with no health problems versus those with one or more problems differentiated the abuse from the accident group at the .01 level ($x^2 = 9.84$). No differences appeared between the high- and lower-certainty abuse subgroups, but the high-certainty subgroup and its matched accident subgroup differed at the .01 level (Fisher's Exact Probability), with the high certainty showing more problems. Thus, in this sample it appears that health problems were characteristic of the entire abuse group at Time One. It is startling that the two groups were very similar as to conditions at birth and as to the injuries that brought them into the study. However, the abused children had accumulated many more health problems than the accident children by Time One.

Developmental evaluations. Ratings of mental development were available for thirteen abused children and seventeen accident children for Time One. About half of each group scored average or above. Ratings of motor development for the same period were available for fourteen abused and seventeen accident children. Twelve accident children were rated average or above compared with only six of the abused children, but this was not a significant difference. Ten of the abused and ten of the accident children were considered average or above average in the development of language, but many of these children were too young for a reliable evaluation.

Behavioral characteristics. Here again, no difference was found between abused and accident children on ratings of either distractibility or activity. Most of the children in both groups were active and moderately distractible. Ratings of mood showed a significant difference between the abused and accident children ($x^2 = 5.95$, $p < .02$): the abused children showed more negative and variable moods than the accident group. This difference was accentuated when the children in the high-certainty abuse subgroup were compared with their accident matches.

Accidents. The results of the accident census are discussed under the findings for Time Two.

The Children: Findings, Time Two

Health. By the time the children were seen again at Time Two, one year later, five of the abused children had been removed from their natural homes by the protective services. Four had been placed in foster homes and one was in an institution for young children. This change in environment probably accounted for the recovery of most of them from the failure-to-thrive as seen at Time One. Table 7 shows anthropometric measures for Time Two and

TABLE 7. Anthropometric Measures for Abused and Accident Children, T_2

	Weight Percentile		Height Percentile		Head Circumference Percentile	
	Mean	Range	Mean	Range	Mean	Range
Abuse (n = 16)[a]	42.82	<3–95	39.18	<3–93	31.77	<3–98
Accident (n = 17)	55.24	<3–>97	59.0	<3–>97	42.06	<3–80

Note: No significant differences between abused and accident children were found.

a. One abusive mother refused to bring her child for the final procedure.

indicates no significant differences between the major groups. Not shown are comparisons for the high-certainty abuse subgroup: these children weighed less, were shorter, and had smaller head circumferences than the children in the matched accident subgroup and those in the lower-certainty subgroup, but only the last-named measure was significantly different.

Table 8 reviews the health problems at Time Two. The Erb's Palsy of one abused child and the arthrogryposis of one accident child had been present from birth. The failure-to-thrive of one of the abused children and the possibility of failure-to-thrive of one of the accident children had not been present at Time One. The cataract of one abused boy probably resulted from injury during the interim between Time One and Time Two. By the time of the

TABLE 8. Health Problems of Abused and Accident Children, T_2

	Abuse (n = 17)	Accident (n = 17)
CNS[a] difficulties only	3	0
CNS plus failure-to-thrive	1	0
Erb's palsy and CNS	1	0
Generally retarded development	1	1
Possible cerebral palsy[b]	1	0
Breath-holding and symptomatic seizures	1	0
Cataract, probably traumatic	1	0
Mild URI[c]	1	1
Asthma and hemiparesis[d]	0	1
Arthrogryposis	0	1
Psychomotor retardation	0	1
Question of failure-to-thrive	0	1

a. Central Nervous System.
b. There was a possibility of arrested hydrocephalus.
c. Upper-Respiratory Infection.
d. Hemiparesis secondary to subdural.

final evaluation, he had been placed in a foster home and appeared to be doing well.

The health problems of the abuse group were considerably more numerous and serious than those of the accident group, particularly in respect to central nervous system difficulties. Seven abused and thirteen accident children were free of health problems at Time Two. The comparable figures at Time One were two and twelve. This improvement in health was probably due to the greater stability of the second year of life and the placement of five abused children in better environments.

Developmental evaluations. At Time Two, evaluations could be conducted for thirteen abused children. One child could not be seen because of his mother's refusal to take part in this last pro- cedure. Three other abused children were so extremely negative that they refused to take tests or even pay attention to the interviewer, and therefore could not be evaluated adequately.[14] Similarly, one accident child refused all tests, leaving sixteen accident children who could be evaluated.

There was no significant difference between the two groups as to mental ratings, although more than half of each group were rated as below average at this time. Slowness in development was especially prominent among the high-certainty abused children; nine of the twelve were judged slow, but this was not significantly different from their accident matches. As at Time One, ratings of motor development tended to favor the accident children, ten of whom were average or above. Only five of the sixteen abused children were rated average or above, but again the difference was not significant. Language evaluation also showed no significant group differences.

The rate of development could be calculated for eight abused and ten accident children, all of whom were scored on the Bayley scales at both Time One and Time Two. The two groups were compared by means of a t-test with the following results:

Abuse group (n = 8) mean = 9.80, s.d. = 2.92
Accident group (n = 10) mean = 9.18, s.d. = 3.91
$t_{16} = 0.37$, N.S.

Since this was a comparison of rate of development for twelve months, the expected score was 12.0. Only one abused child made that much or more progress: 13.8. The abused child who improved the least progressed only 4.3 months (this was the child with arrested hydrocephalus), and the abused child next higher in rate of progress advanced 7.1 months in the year. Two of the accident children made as much or more progress than expected: 15.3 and 12.3 months. The accident child who made the least improvement progressed only .31 months, but this was a child damaged by a difficult birth who had psychomotor retardation at Time Two. The small number of children who had the Bayley test both at Time One and Time Two makes it difficult to draw conclusions, but it is of interest that both groups made so little progress and that there was so little difference between them.

Behavioral characteristics. By Time Two there was no longer a difference in mood between the abused and accident children. Although the abused children were rated approximately the same as at Time One (mostly negative), the accident children had also become negative by Time Two. Activity ratings at Time Two showed that all the abused children were now rated low or moderate in activity whereas the accident children had moved into the high or variable rating ($x^2 = 4.73$, $p < .05$). Measures of distractibility showed that most of the abused group were considered distractible while most of the accident group were not, but the difference was not statistically significant.

Accidents. An accident census was kept between Time One and Time Two by means of interviews, questionnaires, and record review. Every abused child had had at least one accident, but eight of the accident children had suffered none. This proved to be a significant difference ($x^2 = 13.84$, $p < .01$) and raises the question whether the abused children were more clumsy or whether some of them may have sustained additional but unrecognized parental assault.

Nine abused children had suffered two or three accidents and nine accident children had had from one to four. The incidents reported did not seem unusually numerous, but some involved events such as ingesting laquer thinner and being burned by hot water. The second year of life is a period when children are very prone to accidents because of their developing but still uncertain motor skills and their natural curiosity (Gregg and Elmer, 1969). In retrospect, it would have been useful to learn about the circumstances of these accidents; neglect may also have been a factor.

The Families and the Children, Time One–Time Two: A Summary

Before beginning the Infant Accident Study, we had hypothesized that abusive families are subject to more stress of all types than nonabusive families, and that they have fewer emotional supports and would therefore be more vulnerable to stress in their everyday lives. We anticipated that they would provide poorer physical care, would punish more harshly, and would have higher expectations and more negative perception of their children. We also had hypothesized that the abused babies would prove inferior to the nonabused in health, physical and motor development, acquisition of language, and development of cognitive skills, and would show more negative mood. Our hypotheses concerning the mothers were corroborated, for we found substantial differences between abusive and accident mothers. The abusive group had significantly less education and enjoyed less support. They were also less stable; the stress they reported between conception of the index child and the traumatic incident was both different from and greater than that reported by the accident mothers. They also provided poorer overall child care, but no differences were found between the groups as to methods of punishment. Paradoxically, mothers in the abuse group had more realistic expectations concerning the age of learning right from wrong than those in the accident group, but they were more prepared to use physical punishment to enforce this learning. Within the abusive group, two subgroups were defined: high certainty and lower certainty. The high-certainty subgroup was statistically different from the lower-certainty subgroup on several demographic characteristics, had significantly lower overall stability and support scores, and gave poorer child care compared with both the lower-certainty and the relevant accident subgroups.

The children were evaluated at Time One and again at Time Two, one year later. No group differences were found as to birth order or number of children in the family. Adverse birth conditions were evenly distributed among the children in both groups, as were their later traumatic injuries. Although the two groups were virtually indistinguishable at birth, by the time they entered the study the health problems of the abused children far exceeded those of the accident children; only two abused, compared with twelve accident children, were free from health problems. Mean percentiles for weight, height, and head circumference were lower for the abused children, but only the difference in weight was significant. Neurological signs were more prominent in the abuse group.

More than half of each group were rated average or higher in mental development at Time One and no significant differences were found as to mental, motor, or language development. Ratings of activity and distractibility were similar for both groups, but the abused children, especially in the high-certainty group, were more negative in mood. At Time Two, anthropometric measurements for the abused children remained lower than those for the accident children, but the significant difference in weight had disappeared, probably because five of the high-certainty children had been removed from their natural homes and placed in more nurturing environments. The children in the high-certainty subgroup had significantly smaller head sizes than those in their matched accident subgroup. At Time Two the abused children still had poorer health, but both they and the accident children had improved. Again, no group differences appeared in developmental ratings, but more than half of each group were now rated slow in mental development.

The group differences in mood at Time One had disappeared, largely because the accident children had become more negative. They also evidenced more motor activity while the abused group showed less; this resulted in a statistical difference between the two groups. A statistically greater number of abused children had suffered at least one accident, but the role of neglect or abuse in these accidents was not explored. Thus, except for health, our hypotheses concerning the abused children were not corroborated.

Contrary to our expectations, the two groups, which had appeared very different at Time One, seemed quite similar by Time Two. They had coalesced in measures of development and drawn close in anthropometric measures and mood. Perhaps this was due to the effects of social class, which has been found to be a major determinant of the rate and level of child development and is believed to have an impact long before entrance into school. This subject will be discussed more fully in a later section.

CHAPTER 2

The Follow-Up Study

This was the first stage in the attempt to follow the children of the Infant Accident Study through the school years and into early adulthood, marriage, and parenthood. The children were now between eight and a half and nine and a half. We chose to reevaluate them eight years after Time One because they would now be in school but would not yet have reached adolescence, when a variety of other factors could complicate a study.

We hypothesized that the abused children would fall below the nonabused in (1) height and weight, (2) language development, (3) self-concept, (4) intellectual functioning, and (5) ability to empathize, and that the abused children would score higher than the nonabused in (1) number of interim illnesses and injuries, (2) impulsivity, and (3) aggression. Children no longer in the abusive environment, that is, in foster or adoptive homes, were expected to function at a higher level than those who had remained with abusive caretakers, although we made no specific hypotheses. We expected the abusive and accident families to differ as to stability and support, stress, and behavior related to the child because they had differed so much at Time One–Time Two, but we could not formulate hypotheses because about half the abused children were living with substitute families at Time Three. Since the focus of our study was the children, not the families, no attempt was made to evaluate natural families whose children were no longer living with them.

Our hypotheses about the children's current level of development were based on years of clinical observation of many children, our knowledge of the history of the study children, and the few pertinent reports in the literature (Elmer, 1967; Morse et al., 1970; and Martin et al., 1974). The traumatic incident was only one of the insults that had been sustained by the abused children in our study. Many had started life disadvantaged because of low birth weight, had received indifferent or inadequate care, and had been subjected since infancy to a range of health problems. These ills were compounded by severe family problems including instability and lack of support, and the abused children appeared to have a grim outlook for future development. The authors of the three studies cited above all found some degree of physical and mental retardation when children abused in infancy were evaluated at a later time. Other authors have cited malnourishment in infancy (a frequent partner of abuse) as one cause of subsequent smaller size (Birch and Richardson, 1972) and poor school performance (Richardson, Birch, and Hertzig, 1973).

Students of child development and experts in linguistics believe that one of the most important factors in language development is a responsive environment. Some investigators have emphasized early mother-child interaction in their discussions of the development of language (Mahler and Furer, 1963; Mahler, 1968). Church (1961), while recognizing the influence of the mother, believes that linguistic ability stems from the child's efforts to separate from the maternal figure. And the effects on language of a nonstimulating environment have been poignantly described by Spitz (1945) and by Provence and Lipton (1962). Abuse is often accompanied by parental apathy or hostility; these attitudes alone would have a harmful effect on the acquisition of language skills. The children in our sample had been physically traumatized at a time when language was in the very early stages of development and were, therefore, especially vulnerable to adverse influences in this area.

It is likely that the young child who has been abused (and perhaps suffered environmental deprivation) will find it difficult to learn to relate to others and develop an adequate self-concept. When a child is repeatedly the target of adult aggression, he or she may be expected to learn a pattern of relating to others with anxiety, anger, and retaliation. Or he may defend himself by withdrawal and assumed stupidity. Whatever the behavioral manifestation, it seems likely that he views himself as a worthless person.

The seeds of future psychological troubles are thought to be sown in abused children. Although eight- or nine-year-olds are not likely to be identified as delinquent in the legal sense, they may manifest behaviors congruent with delinquency, such as poor impulse control or excessive aggression against persons or property. These behavior patterns often develop because of early feelings of rage and fear in relation to authority figures and because of the instability of the family, implying inconsistency and unpredictability of parents and all authority figures. Owens and Straus (1975) reported that witnessing or experiencing violence during childhood leads to greater tolerance of violence as an adult, and others have pointed out that assassins such as Lee Harvey Oswald and Sirhan Sirhan were grossly mistreated as youngsters (Silver et al., 1969; Fontana, 1973). Still unknown, however, is the proportion of abused children who become violent teen-agers or adults.

The possible abuse sample for the follow-up study consisted of the twenty-four children judged abused at Time Two in the Infant Accident Study. The pool of accident children for matching purposes was made up of the sixty-three so classified at both Time One and Time Two. Children who were classified as abused at Time One but not Time Two were excluded from both the abuse and accident sample, as were children classified at Time Two as neglected only (that is, no accompanying abuse). Accident children were matched to abused children on age, race, sex, and socioeconomic status. It was possible to find matching accident subjects for nineteen abused children; this number was later reduced to seventeen abused and seventeen accident children.[1] Each group consisted of nine blacks (seven males and two females) and eight whites (five males and three females). Of the seventeen abused children, twelve had been classified as high certainty and five as lower certainty. Eight of the high-certainty abused children were also neglected. The children were largely of lower-class background (classes IV and V according to the Hollingshead Two-Factor Index of Social Position).

In addition, we provided an untraumatized comparison group of children who had not been studied before. They were selected from hospital inpatient and outpatient populations and matched to the seventeen abused children on age, race, sex, and socioeconomic status. We also required that there be no history of abuse according to Child Welfare Services records and no history of accident resulting in referral to a hospital before the age of twelve months. Many of the traumatized children had been hospitalized before the age of twelve months because of their injuries. Since hospitalization usually necessitates separation from the mother, and since very young children are considered especially vulnerable to such separation, it seemed possible that any group differences found between traumatized and untraumatized children might be attributable to differences in hospital experience during infancy and its effect on subsequent emotional development (Bowlby, 1969). To avoid such a possibility, we decided to control for this variable.

In nine cases both the abused child and the matching accident child were similar as to infantile hospitalization, that is, either both had been inpatients or neither had been. For each of these pairs we selected one untraumatized comparison child who was matched on early hospital experience as well as on the relevant demographic variables. The members of the remaining eight pairs of traumatized children were dissimilar as to infantile hospitalization. For each of these pairs we selected two comparison children: one matched the abused child as to infantile hospital experience, and the other matched the accident child. Thus, a total of twenty-five comparison children were chosen.

It was difficult to decide which infantile illness leading to hospitalization might provide acceptable comparison children. Some diseases (for example, asthma, meningitis) were considered unsuitable because they are likely to result in overprotection or excessive worry by the mother, thus distorting the parent-child relationship. The decision was to seek out children whose chief complaint upon hospitalization had been an acute infection. Even more difficult to identify were comparison children with only outpatient hospital experience at or before twelve months because hospitals rarely index outpatient visits according to chief complaint. Administrative arrangements had to be made with three hospitals and hundreds of records scanned before the requisite number of matched comparison children could be found. Then a responsible hospital official had to call and request the parents' participation and their consent to release confidential hospital information about themselves and their children before the standard introductory letter could go out and the research interviewers could begin.

Thus, the follow-up study consisted of seventeen abused and seventeen accident children, matched on age, race, sex, and socioeconomic status. Each of these traumatized groups had its own comparison group of untraumatized children matched on the same variables plus early hospital experience. The largest variation in social class, according to the Hollingshead Two-Factor Index of Social Position, was two classes; this difference was not significant. Otherwise, social class matched exactly or was one class apart. The Chi-square test showed no significant difference in class between the groups. In the following analyses, three main comparisons are made: (1) abused children and untraumatized children, matched as to infantile hospital experience; (2) accident children and untraumatized children, matched as to infantile hospitalization; and (3) abused children and accident children. In the third comparison, history of hospitalization could not be matched as nine of the seventeen abused children but only five of the seventeen accident children had been inpatients before the age of twelve months. Comparisons were also made between the high-certainty subgroup of the abused children and its matched accident and untraumatized subgroups.

The Families, Time Three

We had not seen the families in the Infant Accident Study in eight to nine years, although in 1971 a report on the study had been mailed to them. Despite many changes in address and sometimes in name, we were able to locate each of the thirty-four families.[2] No appointments were made by phone since it is easy to refuse a stranger who telephones; instead, each mother received an introductory letter (Appendix 2a), announcing the study and requesting the family's participation. In most instances the interviewers were blind to the group identification of the family, but in eight cases the existence of a substitute mother made blindness impossible.

A black female interviewer saw all the black mothers and a white female interviewer all the whites. We soon found that one stumbling block might be the refusal of the child himself to come for the examination. Several comparison mothers expressed personal willingness but said they could not speak for their young children, who were interested in karate, football, swimming, etc. We therefore added a black male and a white male interviewer with the express purpose of engaging the child in the study firsthand. The female interviewer talked to the mother while the male interviewer attempted to make friends with the child through puzzles or games.

Early in the interview the mother was asked to read and sign the consent form, which was also explained sentence by sentence. In addition, she signed permissions for the gathering of information from schools, medical sources, and social agencies. The structured interview covered demographic data, separations of the child or others from the rest of the family, the mother's health, and methods of reward and punishment. Following evaluation of the child we informed the mother about the results and referred her to other agencies if indicated. In some instances final discussions with the mother lasted through several home visits. Mothers were given a small amount of compensation plus carfare; children were also given a token amount.

As in the Infant Accident Study, groups of families were compared as to demographic characteristics, stability, support, and the mother's behavior in relation to the index child (child care, methods of punishment and reward, and perception of the child). The variables used to analyze the Time One–Time Two and Time

Three data were identical and the scoring was also the same, apart from some exceptions which will be discussed below.

Of the original twelve high-certainty abuse families, eight were no longer caring for the index children. Five of the children were now in long-term foster homes[3] and three others had been adopted. Thus, only four high-certainty families were still living with their index children. These four high-certainty families were combined with the five low-certainty families to form a group of abusive families (n = 9). These nine abusive families were compared with their matched accident (n = 9) and matched comparison families (n = 9), and with the foster and adoptive families (n = 8). We also compared the seventeen accident mothers with the seventeen mothers of untraumatized children.

Demographic characteristics. The four groups discussed above were compared at Time Three on the basis of the mother's age, race, marital status, living status, education, and employment status; on the income per month per person; and on the family's socioeconomic status.

Stability. The stability index at Time Three consisted of the same seven items as at Time One–Time Two:

1. The mother's living status.
2. Adequacy of income.[4]
3. Source of income (that is, from a job or other private source, as opposed to welfare).
4. Number of family moves. The basis was the number of moves during the previous five years, since families of school-age children are thought to be less mobile.
5. The mother's health.[5]
6. Amount of family stress.[6]
7. Continuity of the family's care of the index child.[7]

The seven items were analyzed individually, after which their scores were combined to yield an overall stability rating. The higher the score, the more stable the family was considered. (For the scoring system for these seven items, see Appendix 2b.)

Support. The support index for Time Three assessed the role of seven possible sources of support: (1) husband or boyfriend, (2) immediate family members, (3) extended family, (4) unrelated individuals, (5) religion, (6) professionals, and (7) other groups (clubs, societies, unions, etc.).[8] (The chart for sources of support, supportive activities, and scoring can be found in Appendix 2c.)

Mother's behavior in relation to the child. Three aspects of child-related behavior were examined:

1. Child care. The quality of child care at Time Three was judged on the bases of completeness of immunizations, dental condition and frequency of visits to the dentist, and the child's physical appearance. The pediatrician's findings were converted into ratings on the basis of carefully defined criteria for each of the three aspects of child care. A physician and a research assistant developed the criteria, then worked together to rate each child on each aspect.[9]

2. Attitudes toward punishment and maternal expectations of the child. During the home interview, mothers were asked how they would respond to the following situations: a child's missing school without good reason, poor school performance, forgetfulness with respect to right from wrong, destruction of property, lying, hitting the mother, acting "upset," and engaging in dangerous practices such as lighting matches.[10] We also asked at what age the child had learned right from wrong. (The chart developed for child offenses and maternal reactions is shown in Appendix 2d.) The analysis permitted assessment of the number of child offenses that the mothers regarded as punishable, the number of punishments used by each mother, and an approximation of the ratio of appropriate to inappropriate maternal reactions for offenses related to school and for other offenses. We also inquired how their disciplinary practices compared with those of their own parents.

3. Perception of the child. As mentioned in chapter 2, distorted maternal perception of abused children has been reported by various authors. In the follow-up study the mothers' spontaneous comments about the index child, in addition to replies to routine questions during the pediatric history, were recorded and judged as positive, negative, or neutral.[11] To obtain a more systematic assess-

ment of maternal perception of the child, a brief questionnaire, "Your Child — Most Children" was developed (Appendix 2e).[12]

We examined pregnancy and birth records for all comparison mothers in order to have data comparable to those gathered for the mothers of traumatized children. Perinatal stress scores were calculated using the Werner system (1967). Data from social agencies and other institutions were also collected to provide as much collateral information as possible. To ensure comparable data, standard outlines were sent to each agency.

The Families: Findings

Demographic characteristics. Table 9 shows demographic characteristics for the four groups of families at Time Three. The only significant difference was in the greater age of the substitute mothers. This reflects the fact that many foster mothers are drawn from the pool of older mothers whose natural families have grown up and departed from the household.

At Time Three the accident families had a lower income per person than any of the other groups, though not at a significant level. Two of the abusive mothers and three or four of the mothers from each of the other groups were working. (It will be recalled that none of the mothers were working at Time One.) For the most part, the women's jobs were fairly routine and low paid (day work, clerk, kitchen help). In contrast, the two abusive mothers held responsible, well-paid jobs, for example, executive secretary. A few men in each group had better jobs at Time Three than at Time One. Some had found new jobs or had been promoted, for example, from key puncher to computer programmer. Promotions of this kind of course meant substantially higher salaries. Some other men who had been living on welfare aid at Time One had by Time Three received specialized training and found jobs. The fathers showing the least improvement were those in the accident group. The period from 1966 (when we began to see children in the Infant Accident Study) to 1974 (the time of the follow-up) was a generally

TABLE 9. Demographic Characteristics of Natural Abusive,

	Age[a]		Race		Marital Status		Living Status	
	Mean (Yrs.)	Range (Yrs.)	Black	White	Married	Other[b]	With Someone[c]	Alone
Natural abusive (n = 9)	34.6	29–47	3	6	6	3	6	3
Matched accident (n = 9)	36.1	31–42	3	6	5	4	5	4
Matched comparison (n = 9)	34.0	26–46	3	6	6	3	6	3
Substitute (n = 8)	46.4	24–66	6	2	7	1	8	0

a. The age of the substitute mothers was significantly greater ($t_{15} = 2.57$, $p < .05$).
b. "Other" includes single, separated, divorced, or widowed.

prosperous time, and it seemed strange that these fathers were, on the whole, less able than those in the other groups to take advantage of the economic situation.

In twelve cases the improved status of the jobs resulted in shifting family socioeconomic status upward. The families moving up were about equally divided among all the groups. In one instance, socioeconomic status improved by two classes, but most shifts were from class V to class IV (or from very low to low). And in each group except the abusive one, one or two families had declined in socioeconomic status. Overall, at Time Three the groups remained comparable as to socioeconomic status and two-thirds of the families were still in classes IV and V. As previously discussed, we were matching on the basis of child characteristics and the only characteristic on which families were matched was socioeconomic class. Therefore, it came as a surprise that the natural, abusive, accident, and comparison groups were all remarkably similar in

Matched Accident, Matched Comparison, and Substitute Mothers, T₃

Education		Employment		Income per Month (Per Person)		Socioeconomic Status				
< High School	≥ High School	Working or Student	Unem- ployed	Mean	Range	I	II	III	IV	V
3	6	4	5	$164.47	$60–$350	0	2	1	4	2
1	8	5	4	$101.73	$60–$140	0	1	2	3	3
3	6	4	5	$166.48	$60–$366	0	0	4	4	1
3	5	4	4	$159.82	$30–$366	0	0	1	4	3

c. "With Someone" includes living with husband, boyfriend, relatives, or friends.

many of their demographic characteristics.

At Time Three all seventeen accident mothers and the mothers in the untraumatized comparison group seemed very similar, and no significant differences appeared. Therefore, from this point on, results will not be presented for the full group of accident mothers and their comparison group. Inasmuch as the abusive group is the group of interest, this account will concentrate on the abusive mothers and their experiences. The only exception is the reporting of the results of the questionnaire "Your Child — Most Children" in a later section.

Stability. The assessment of stability showed no differences between the natural abusive and any of the other three groups except in regard to the mother's health. Health of the foster mothers was considered at less risk for child care than that of the abusive mothers, but this was not statistically significant. The stability scores, of which the highest possible was 14, follow:

Scores	Natural Abusive (n = 9)	Accident (n = 9)	Comparison (n = 9)	Foster/ Adoptive (n = 8)
Range	7–12	3–14	7–14	9–14
Mean	10.22	9.94	10.33	11.75

Support.   The support scores were as follows:

Scores	Natural Abusive (n = 9)	Accident (n = 9)	Comparison (n = 9)	Foster/ Adoptive (n = 8)
Range	3–19	1.5–18	5–20	13–18
Mean	10.83	10.61	12.89	14.81

The substitute mothers had greater support, but not at a significant level. The highest possible score was 20. Support for Time Three was not analyzed by items because of the more detailed index that was used.[13]

We were interested in assessing the benefits for those abused children who had moved into substitute care by Time Three. We subtracted the stability scores of the natural abusive families at Time One from the stability scores of the substitute families caring for the same children at Time Three. The same procedure was followed for the rest of the natural abusive families at Time One and at Time Three (these were the families still caring for their children). The change in stability was greater for the children who had moved into substitute care ($t_{15} = 3.82$, $p < .01$) and was in a positive direction. We compared the same groups for change in support between Time One and Time Three. The substitute homes provided significantly greater support ($t_{14} = 2.73$, $p < .02$). (The family of one child could not be assessed on this variable.)

Mother's behavior in relation to the child.   The following results were established from studying the three aspects of this variable:

1. Child care. No differences were found between the groups for any of the aspects rated: immunizations, dental care, or physical child care. The mothers in the entire sample were doing well with

immunizations. About half the natural abusive mothers were doing poorly as to dental care; the comparisons had a better record but not at a significant level. Physical child care was uniformly good across the entire sample.

2. Attitudes toward punishment and maternal expectations of the child. The Time One–Time Two expectations as to the age of learning right from wrong were equally divided between less than one year of age and one year of age and older. By Time Three the mothers were reporting actual experience and most said their children had learned this distinction by the age of two. The mothers (natural and substitute) of the high-certainty abused children were significantly different from their matched accident mothers (Fisher's Exact Probability, $p = .05$). They perceived that their children had learned right from wrong when more than two years of age, while the accident mothers felt such learning had occurred at less than two years.

As to punishment, maternal reactions at Time Three ranged from ignoring the behavior through verbal criticism, deprivation of privileges, and isolation, to physical punishment. The mothers were divided almost equally as to the number of different punishments used. Half used four or fewer types and half gave five or more. The number of offenses that the mother would meet by physical punishment again divided the group almost equally, and ranged from one to six. Nineteen of the mothers said that one or two different kinds of offenses would merit physical punishment; sixteen mothers would physically punish for three to six different kinds of offenses. However, these differences were not related to group identification.

One accident mother described becoming progressively enraged as she beat her son. At the end, in a final surge of fury, she wanted to kill him. Several other mothers who spoke of extremely harsh disciplinary measures appeared to feel little guilt or regret. Indeed, several parents walloped their children in the presence of interviewers. Mrs. C., angry because her five-year-old had neglected to wash, slapped the child, then looked for a belt to beat her. The child escaped more severe punishment only because no belt was available. Mothers were also asked about the methods of punishment they used compared with those used by their own parents. Across the whole sample, mothers tended to use the same kinds of punishment as their parents, but said they themselves were not so harsh. For example, Mrs. C. had been beaten regularly by her own parents, who "never talked" to her.

We examined the number of inappropriate maternal responses to school situations and found such responses were about equal across all groups and about half of each group exhibited responses we deemed inappropriate. One mother paid her child to attend school because he disliked it so intensely and complained of shortness of breath and headaches to avoid going. Several mothers often kept their children out of school to go on shopping trips and babysit for younger siblings. Inappropriate responses to problems other than school were also equally spread among the various groups. For example, one mother said she would break a toy or game of her son's if he destroyed property.

3. Perception of the child. At Time One–Time Two we had found no group differences in maternal perception, which was generally extremely positive. At Time Three there were no differences between the groups, but now more than half of each group were rated as predominantly negative or neutral in their spontaneous comments and answers to systematic questions concerning the index child. One mother called her eight-year-old daughter a "sexpot," and another complained that her son "cried whenever she looked at him cross-eyed." This procedure did not directly address the question of whether abusive mothers had a distorted perception of the child, as reported by several investigators and previously noted. If negative perceptions lead to negative behavior, however, the results suggest that half the children in our total sample were being reared in environments that were indifferent or even hostile to them. A follow-up study of twenty-five abused or neglected children (Morse et al., 1970) found that only six children were developing normally. Five of these had mothers who described them in positive terms. The gross disturbance of seven other children was associated with their mothers' negative percep-

tion of them. We have no scientific explanation for the change in the mothers' perceptions between Time One–Time Two and Time Three. Perhaps the problems associated with child-rearing become more burdensome as the child becomes more independent and the parents become older and more weighed down by the various stresses of everday life.

We examined the responses to the "Your Child—Most Children" questionnaire according to the original groups of children. All the caretakers of the abused children, whether foster, adoptive, or natural, were grouped together. Their responses were compared with those of the accident mothers and with those of their comparison group. We also compared responses of the accident mothers with those of their comparison group. Caretakers of the seventeen abused children saw their offspring as angrier than most children of the same age; this was not true of their untraumatized comparison group. According to the Z statistic, this finding was significant at less than the .05 level.

Mothers of accident children thought that their offspring tended to be more persevering than other children; this was significantly different from the mothers in the comparison group ($p < .05$). Mothers of accident children also saw their offspring as more exploratory in relation to the environment than most other children; this was significantly different from the perception of the caretakers of abused children ($p < .05$).

The Children, Time Three

The mothers brought their children to the laboratory for a half day of evaluations. The children were assessed as to health; language and hearing; impulsivity, aggression, and empathy; perceptual-motor coordination; self-concept; and motor activity. All clinicians were qualified specialists who were blind to the group identification of the children. In addition, the children were examined on the basis of school ability and achievement; clinical assessments of their ability to control aggression and the degree of psychological disturbance, based on the entire written protocol;

and child-outcome and predictor variables. The last procedure will be explained more fully in a later section.

Records were collected from the child welfare agency in any county where a contact had been made with either the child or his family. After discussing the purpose of our study with agency officials, we sent them an outline of the desired information, which related to past and present placements of the child or siblings away from home and contacts of the child welfare service with the child and his natural family. We also requested an assessment of the present environment and of the child (health, behavior, intellectual progress).

Demographic characteristics.   At Time Three our study contained seventeen abused and seventeen accident children and a comparison group of twenty-five untraumatized children matched to the abuse/accident pairs on the basis of age, race, sex, socioeconomic status, and infant hospitalization. The children ranged in age from eight years, eight months, to nine years, six months, and the greatest mean difference in age between the groups was 4.47 months. The subgroup of interest was the twelve high-certainty abused children, of whom five had been placed in foster homes and three adopted.

Health.   This characteristic was assessed by means of a pediatric examination that included anthropometric measures, a systems review (for example, gastrointestinal), and attention to gross neurological signs and behavioral symptoms. Another physician and a research assistant converted these raw data into scales measuring five aspects of health: operations and hospitalizations, other illnesses and injuries, neurological signs, systems review, and allergies.[14] A pediatric health history was obtained from the mother, who was seen *after* the child to ensure blindness with respect to substitute mothers. We also collected the pregnancy and birth records for the untraumatized comparison group and calculated their perinatal stress scores (Werner et al., 1967).

Language and hearing.   The language evaluation was performed by an experienced speech pathologist. It consisted of ratings of expressive language as well as ratings of articulation under two conditions: testing and conversation. Articulation during testing was assessed by means of selected portions of the picture test section of the Arizona Articulation Proficiency Scale, Revised (Fudala, 1970); articulation during conversation was scored on the basis of the child's responses to the Blacky cards (Blum, 1950), which were used only to elicit stories and not to explore personality dynamics. Another technique to draw out expressive language was the presentation by the examiner of five stimulus situations (not shown in an appendix) about which the child was asked to make up stories.

The formal articulation test was scored as the child responded to each item during the testing session.[15] The examiner accepted as correct all typical Pittsburgh regional variations as well as black dialectical variations. The basic vocabulary unit from the Stanford-Binet (Terman and Merrill, 1960) was presented to obtain a measure of the child's ability to deal with verbal items in a standardized intelligence test.

Hearing was tested bilaterally by means of a Maico portable audiometer using frequencies in the speech range at 25 dB (Anderson, 1972). A child failed the screening if he or she demonstrated two or more failures in the speech range. This test was designed to guard against rating a child low on the language tests when he might actually be handicapped by poor hearing.

Impulsivity, aggression, and empathy. Impulsivity was defined as the extent to which a person gives in to feelings, thoughts, and needs of the moment without thinking through the situation and assessing the best course of action. Aggression was defined as behavior that aims to inflict injury or pain upon others; a coercive use of power to manipulate or harm oneself or others; or defending oneself against undue pressure, harm, or coercion. Aggression may be expressed in verbal, nonverbal, or physical ways. Empathy was defined as the capacity to view events from the standpoint of others. The traits were evaluated by the analysis of stories invented and acted out by the children in response to five stimulus paragraphs (Appendix 3a). Puppets were utilized to encourage greater latitude for the expression of fantasy, for puppetry, along with storytelling, role-playing, and a variety of other expressive media, has a long-established place in diagnostic and therapeutic work with children (among others, see Woltmann, 1940, 1960; Rambert, 1949; and Haworth, 1968). It is assumed that children use puppets as a projective device, revealing their inner conflicts and wishes as they weave a story around puppet characters (Ekstein, 1965; Irwin and Shapiro, 1975). An expressive-arts clinician, experienced in work with children, had developed the stimulus paragraphs and tested them on twenty children not in this study. The paragraphs elicited a variety of rich fantasy material that lent itself to ratings of the behavioral characteristics in question (see Appendices 3b–3d for examples). Prior to this follow-up study, scale points for the scoring of the protocols were defined and reliability of the judges was established at a satisfactory level. (Rating scales for the characteristics of impulsivity, aggression, and empathy can be found in Appendix 3e.)

To begin the procedure, the child was brought to a medium-sized room containing a small stage. After being greeted by the clinician, he or she was instructed to go behind the stage and asked to make up endings to the stories that would be told and to play out each story. The clinician sat in front of the stage, handed the child a doll or a puppet suitable for the story, and then read the stimulus paragraph. At the end of the fifth story, the clinician suggested that the child make up a story of his own. For this he had his choice of all the dolls and puppets, which were spread out on the floor.

At the conclusion of the spontaneous story the clinician inquired about parts that might not be clear and posed standard questions concerning the name of the story, the characters whom the child preferred or disliked, and the lesson or moral. The entire session was tape-recorded and the clinician also took verbatim notes. The stories were then transcribed, separated, and coded according to a random table in order to scramble subjects and stories.[16]

Psychological tests. The Bender Gestalt Test (Koppitz, 1964) was administered to obtain an impression of the children's perceptual-motor coordination. Self-concept was assessed by the

Piers-Harris Self Concept Scale (Piers and Harris, 1970).[17] This test has been widely used on children of approximately the same age as our subjects.

Motor activity. It was considered important to assess motor activity because minimal brain damage is thought to be associated with hyperactivity. Although only a few children were known to have suffered head injuries, blows to the head or shaking might have caused subtle, unrecognized damage. We were also interested in obtaining a measure of motor activity at this age since the traumatized children had had two previous ratings as infants, one at Time One and one at Time Two.

Motor activity was measured by telemetric bands wrapped around each wrist and ankle. Any movement — arm, leg, finger, toe — was signaled to a synchronized receiver in an observation booth, which automatically tallied movements as they occurred. Although the procedure had been used with adults, this was the first time it had been utilized for children. The electronic monitoring was far more accurate than the observer's tallies at Time One and Time Two.[18] Activity was measured while the child was responding to the Piers-Harris Self Concept Scale, the Rod Slide and Dynamometer Test (not analyzed for this report), the Bender Gestalt, and a ten-minute period of free play that began at the conclusion of the formal tests when the examiner removed a screen revealing twelve attractive toys, then left the room. The child was free to use whatever toys he wished during the ten minutes.

Throughout the tests and free play a staff member in the observation booth described what the child was doing, using an event recorder that was synchronized with the four receivers tallying the child's motor activity. The groups were compared on activity measures for each of the procedures outlined above, for the right and left wrists, for the right ankle, and for whole body activity. Comparisons were also made according to neurological scores.

School ability and achievement. Special efforts were made to obtain copies of all school records. We requested current and past grades and grade placements, achievement- and psychological-test results, and attendance and health records. All information was requested for the child's entire school experience, which at this point had averaged about three years.

School data formed the basis for assessing intellectual ability and performance for the entire sample of children. A psychologist, blind to the child's classification, who was familiar with the different school systems and with the tests commonly used, examined all the school data for each child. Reports on psychological tests and on formal tests of ability were the basis for rating each child's ability, and grade placements and grades on tests of subject matter (for example, reading) formed the basis for rating his achievement. Both ability and achievement were rated as below average, average, or above. The ratio of achievement to ability provided information as to the child's intellectual progress in relation to his capacity.

Since the children were scattered in a number of different school systems in western Pennsylvania, we anticipated that the kind of data we would obtain would be variable, to say the least. A teacher questionnaire (see Appendix 3f), modeled on the one used by Werner, Bierman, and French (1971) was therefore developed to obtain systematic information on all the children.[19] Teacher questionnaires have been reported as excellent sources of information about children's day-to-day performance (Richardson et al., 1973). The teacher was asked to rate the child as less than average, average, or above average on a number of qualities related to school performance, for example, attention span and interest in school. The teacher also indicated the presence or absence of particular language difficulties and specified behavior problems such as irritability or overly aggressive behavior. Finally, a list of nervous habits was included for the teacher to comment upon when applicable to the child.

Clinical assessment of behavior.   All records, both past and current, were summarized in writing for each child. These included our interview data and follow-up test results, school reports, and reports from other medical sources and social agencies. Possible comments about abuse were eliminated from the summaries, as were all data which might identify the child. This information formed the basis for clinical assessments of behavior which were made by a professor of psychiatry and pediatrics, an experienced social worker, and another professional person experienced in work with mental health problems of children. These assessments were made some months after the children had been seen. Children were rated as to control of aggression: under, over, or about average. They were also rated as to probable degree of disturbance on a five-point scale from 1, very disturbed, to 5, no disturbance.

Description or reference to nervous mannerisms was collected for each child from the teacher questionnaires and also from the pediatric screenings.

The Children: Findings

Demographic characteristics. As mentioned earlier, at Time Three the study group comprised seventeen abused children with their untraumatized comparisons and seventeen accident children with their untraumatized comparisons, making a total sample of fifty-nine children. In both cases the comparison children matched the traumatized children as to infantile hospitalization as well as the other relevant variables. The subgroup of interest was the twelve high-certainty abused children, of whom eight were living in substitute homes by Time Three.

Health. Anthropometric measures for the seventeen abused children, the seventeen accident children, and their respective comparisons are presented in table 10. The measures were similar for all groups except that the abused children weighed significantly more than their matched untraumatized comparisons and the high-certainty abused children both were significantly heavier than their matched untraumatized comparisons ($t_{22} = 2.42$, $p < .05$) and tended to be taller. These findings were contrary to expectations. Since eight of the high-certainty children had been in substitute homes for some years, comparison was made of anthropometric measures for them versus the abused children still in their natural homes (table 11). It can be seen that abused children in their natural homes had apparently thrived as well physically as

TABLE 10. Anthropometric Measures for Abused,
Accident, and Comparison Groups, T_3

	Weight Percentile[a]		Height Percentile		Head Circumference Percentile	
	Mean	Range	Mean	Range	Mean	Range
Abuse (n = 17)	41.2	<3–96	48.6	4–97	56.4	25–95
Abuse comparisons (n = 17)	21.5	<3–96	33.4	<3–96	49.3	4–90
Accident (n = 17)	42.9	<3–96	43.1	<3–97	56.4	5–95
Accident comparisons (n = 17)	28.5	<3–>97	33.7	<3–97	56.0	25–>97

a. The abused children were significantly heavier than their untraumatized comparison group (t_{32} = 2.01, $p < .05$). No other statistical results related to this table were significant.

TABLE 11. Anthropometric Measures
for Abused Children in Substitute and Natural Homes, T_3

	Weight Percentile		Height Percentile		Head Circumference Percentile[a]	
	Mean	Range	Mean	Range	Mean	Range
Foster/ adoptive (n = 8)	36.1	<3–96	50.6	20–80	44.1	25–75
Natural (n = 9)	45.7	<3–95	46.8	4–>97	68.1	30–98

a. The foster/adoptive children had significantly smaller head circumferences than the abused children in their natural homes (t_{15} = 2.19, $p < .05$). No other statistical results related to table 11 were significant.

those placed away from home. This is contrary to earlier findings of this author regarding other abused children in which all ten of the children living in different environments were average in height and weight, but six of the ten in their natural homes were below average (Elmer, 1967). No ready explanation comes to mind for the difference in outcome between the subjects of the previous study and those of the present investigation. We did find, however, that the children in substitute care in the follow-up study had a significantly smaller head size than the abused children in their natural homes (table 11). Martin et al. (1974) noted that the rate of head growth after intervention is an indicator to be watched for long-term prognosis.

The raw data for injuries and illnesses showed that the seventeen abused children had a greater number of such occurrences than their untraumatized comparisons, while the accident children exceeded both their untraumatized comparisons and the abused children. The only significant difference, however, was accident versus untraumatized ($\chi^2 = 9.14$, $p < .05$). No differences on this variable appeared between the twelve high-certainty children and either of their comparison groups.

Ten children were considered to have moderate to severe neurological problems. Five were in the abuse group (four of these were high certainty), four in the accident, and one in the comparison group. The only significant difference was between the high-certainty abuse subgroup and their untraumatized matches ($\chi^2 = 4.14$, $p < .05$).

Four of these ten children (two abused and two accident) had had an exceedingly difficult delivery, birth injuries, or congenital anomalies which were followed by continuing difficulties attributable to both their physical condition and the lack of a nurturing environment. One abused child had suffered a traumatic cataract between Time One and Time Two, implying head injury. Two other abused children with poor neurological functioning had no known head injury, birth difficulty, or congenital handicap, but had shown failure-to-thrive at either Time One or Time Two.

A comparison of perinatal stress scores for all the traumatized children versus all the untraumatized comparison children showed a significant association between high perinatal stress (scores of 2 or 3) and later trauma ($\chi^2 = 9.04$, $p < .01$). It may be speculated that children who are difficult to carry or deliver or have neonatal troubles are more vulnerable to lapses in child care (accident) or parental assault at a later time.

No differences appeared between any of the groups as to ratings for systems review or operations and hospitalizations. Likewise, the presence of allergies did not distinguish any group. An interesting serendipitous finding was the unexpected extent of allergies throughout the entire sample of fifty-nine children: 24 percent were subject to one or more of a long list of allergies or allergic manifestations, for example, asthma, hay fever, hives, and sensitivity to food or plants. According to the chief of the allergy department of Children's Hospital of Pittsburgh, the expected incidence of allergies in the hospital population approximates 10 percent. The percentage of children with allergies in another urban population (Philadelphia) has been tentatively reported as 25 percent (Krogman, 1970). Thus, our sample had more allergies than a large pediatric population in this community, but was similar to a far larger population of children in the same state. The significance of this finding is unclear.

Asthma was a problem for seven children or 12 percent of our sample. (Asthmatic children were also counted among those with allergies.) This contrasts with the figure of 2.8 percent reported for schoolchildren in Houston, Texas, another urban area (Smith, 1974). Although asthma has been categorized as a disease with strong emotional overtones, we were unable to find associations between it and any of these indicators of emotional problems: clinical ratings of overcontrolled or undercontrolled aggression, estimated degree of disturbance, or tallies of nervous mannerisms.

Ear problems, for example, otitis media, were also common across the entire follow-up sample. About 50 percent of the fifty-nine children either had drainage tubes in their ears or had recently suffered acute attacks. Ear pathology is frequent among preschool children but usually diminishes at about the age of our sample. The existing conditions were not associated with lack of health care as the majority appeared to enjoy adequate medical attention.

Language and hearing. Because of mechanical failures, three children could not be rated on expressive language; the same children and three others had no ratings of articulation (could not be understood). For the entire tested sample, ratings of articulation during testing were compared with ratings during conversation, and no significant association was found (n = 53; $r = .10$). Most children articulate well in a test situation but have more trouble in normal conversation, so this lack of association was expected. Since conversational articulation is the more important skill, this rating was used for our analyses.

Mean length of utterance was calculated, after which the results were correlated with ratings for expressive language. A high correlation was found (n = 51, $r = .89$, $p < .01$), indicating that this objective measure supported the subjective judgment concerning expressive language skills. (The mean length of utterance of two children could not be evaluated because the tape recorder broke.)

We found a surprising number of language difficulties across the entire sample of children. Seventy percent of the fifty-nine children had one or more language problems. Thirty-nine percent of those who could be rated were poor or very poor in expressive language; 57 percent were poor or very poor in conversational articulation; and 45 percent demonstrated other communication problems including chronic hoarseness, intermittent aphonia (inability to speak), and stuttering. The last figure is of particular interest since the kinds of communication problems represented are widely believed to be associated with tension and anxiety. This aspect of communication by abused children had not been studied before.

The groups were compared as to expressive language, articulation during conversation, other communication disorders, and combinations of these ratings. No differences were found between the abused, accident, and comparison groups, a finding that ran distinctly counter to expectations. Since the whole group of abused children had been traumatized either prior to the acquisition of language or at the time that language was being developed, and since they were also presumably subject to poor family relationships, we had hypothesized that they would be more deficient in language than either the accident children or their untraumatized comparisons.

Comparisons among the subgroups did reveal significant differences. The children in the high-certainty subgroup had poorer ratings of expressive language than both their matched accident and matched untraumatized subgroups (both Fisher's Exact Probability, $p = .05$). They also tended to have poorer ratings than the lower-certainty abuse subgroup, but this was not significant. In every language test children in their own homes did better than those in substitute homes. Two of the results showed the same significant difference (Fisher's Exact Probability, $p = .025$): children in their own homes scored better in conversational articulation and had fewer communication problems. This could be associated with the greater number of health problems at Time One of the foster/ adoptive children, including undernutrition, or with the extremely poor early environment that was a factor in the official decision to place them out of their homes. Although removal to other homes may have been helpful in some respects, for example, the greater stability of the substitute mothers, with respect to language placement apparently came too late or should have been supplemented by other measures. Goldfarb (1945) has reported that placement in substitute homes resulted in substantial recovery from most difficulties but not from language deficiencies.

But another explanation for the differences in language between abused foster/adoptive children and abused children in their own homes is equally plausible. Aside from the high-certainty and lower-certainty subgroups, foster/adoptive and natural-home children were the only groups not matched on race and socioeconomic status. Six of the eight children in substitute care were lower-class black children, while six of the nine children in natural homes were white; four of the latter were middle class. Analyses of expressive language and conversational articulation among all fifty-nine children according to socioeconomic status showed that both skills were significantly associated with social status: more children in the lower classes (IV and V) were rated poor or very poor on expressive language and/or articulation ($\chi^2 = 8.32$, $p < .01$; $\chi^2 = 8.77$, $p < .01$). Other investigators (for example, Bernstein, 1959) have also found that poorer language skills are a concomitant of lower class. Analyses of the same skills by race indicated that whites had significantly better expressive language ($\chi^2 = 6.93$, $p < .01$). Although ratings of articulation favored whites, the difference was not significant.

Favorable expressive language scores in the whole sample were significantly related to higher raw scores on the Binet item of verbal intelligence (Pearson product-moment correlation, $r = .66$, $p < .01$) and to the estimates of intelligence based on the raw scores ($r = .63$, $p < .01$). Skill in expressive language was also related to weight at Time One. This analysis was performed for twenty-eight abused and accident children. Twenty of these had one or more language difficulties at Time Three, and eight had none. The association with weight at Time One was significant ($t_{26} = 2.11$, $p < .05$): those doing better in language at Time Three had weighed more at Time One.

Seven children failed the hearing screening; this was not considered a large proportion. Two were abused, two were accident, and three were comparison children. Only one of the failing children had ear problems, and no association was apparent between failures on hearing tests and expressive language or articulation.

Impulsivity, aggression, and empathy. There were no group differences on any of these variables considering either the mean score for each story or means across all stories. On the variable of empathy there was a sex-based difference, with the girls showing more. Further analyses of the ratings produced only four significant differences, three comparing the seventeen abused children with their matched accident children and one comparing the children in the high-certainty abuse subgroup with their matched accident children. The first significant finding was that the seventeen abused children showed a greater increase in aggression between stories one and six than did their matched accident children ($p = .05$). The second finding was that the abused children showed a greater increase in impulsivity between stories one and five

($p = .03$). The third was that the abused children revealed a greater difference in the pattern of impulsivity from stories one to six ($p = .04$). The fourth significant result showed that the high-certainty abuse subgroup increased more than its matched accident subgroup on ratings of impulsivity between stories one and five ($p = .01$).

These results are difficult to interpret. On one hand, marked increases in aggression and impulsivity under the pressure of ongoing provocative situations could well be one of the characteristics that distinguish abused from nonabused children; the consistency of the findings would seem to support this possibility. On the other hand, no differences appeared between the major abuse group and its untraumatized comparisons; also, the percentage of significant findings was small compared with the number of tests on this material. The conclusion is equivocal: these findings may be no more than chance but may also represent a fertile lead for exploration with a larger number of children.

Psychological results. Since one abused child could not attempt the Bender, the number for abused children was 16. The number of Bender errors distinguished only the high-certainty subgroup from the lower, with the high-certainty making more errors ($t_{14} = 2.27$, $p < .05$). This appears to be a reflection of the difference in neurological findings between the two groups (although this difference did not reach a significant level). Considering only the high-certainty abused children, those with neurological problems made between nine and sixteen errors, while six of the seven with fair to good neurological ratings made from five to eight errors. The seventh child, although considered fair neurologically, made eighteen errors. The results are understood to indicate poorer perceptual-motor coordination among the children of the high-certainty abuse subgroup, but only in comparison to the lower-certainty subgroup.

The results of the Piers-Harris Self Concept Test showed no differences between any of the groups on any of the six scales. The highest possible score was 80 and the actual range was 29–78. The child who scored 78 was Joe, a black male aged eight and a half, one of the children in the comparison group. According to his scores on the individual scales, Joe saw no area in which he was doing poorly. It is of interest to compare Joe's view of himself with the staff's impression of him. He was seen as shy and pleasant, interested in the procedures but generally immature. The pediatric data showed he was in good health and his mother reported that he liked school and did good work. Language skills, however, were assessed as borderline, and three of the examiners commented on Joe's hoarseness and poor voice quality. The fact that inferior communication skills did not depress Joe's positive self-concept is understandable in the light of other information collected during the study. We learned that the schools were dealing with so many children with language and communication difficulties that teachers had become insensitive to the problem and rarely called it to the child's attention, much less suggesting remedial action.

Another comparison child made the lowest score on the self-concept scale, 29. Tim was a white male, almost nine years old, who could find very little to admire in himself. He presented himself as a solemn, anxious, volatile child, constantly fidgeting and jumping about. It was hard for him to attend to any of the procedures. Tim was the middle of five children who together seemed too much for the harried mother to cope with. The mother spoke of Tim as though she scarcely could distinguish him from her other children. One act that did get her attention was Tim's attack on a neighbor child with a knife.

Motor activity. Comparisons of tallies of motor activity were made for each sequence of the testing procedure — for each wrist, for the right ankle, and for the total body (combination of wrists and right ankle). Delays in installation and malfunctioning of the equipment reduced the total number of children whose motor activity could be measured. We also eliminated from the analysis the ten children with poor neurological functioning. The best comparison measure was judged to be the total body activity during free play. This showed that the accident children had significantly greater motor activity than the abuse group $(t_{22} = 2.37, p < .05)$. The abused children were less active than their matched comparisons, but not significantly so.

As was discussed earlier, at Time Two the abused children had also been rated significantly lower in activity than the accident group. Findings of lowered activity among abused children are congruent with reports from Galdston (1965). The high activity of the accident group is consistent with their mothers' descriptions, showing them to be more persevering and more curious than other children of the same age.

School ability and achievement. We examined ability according to school tests, achievement in school, and the ratio of achievement to ability. Ability ratings across the sample, combining the untraumatized comparisons, were as follows:

	< *Average*	*Average*	> *Average*
Abuse	4	10	3
Accident	3	14	0
Combined comparisons	3	20	2

Two facts stand out: three abused children, 18 percent of the group, had better than average ability. The number of abused children in our sample was much smaller that that in the sample examined by Martin et al. (1974), and our methods of assessing ability were different. Nevertheless, our results were similar in finding a relatively normal distribution of intellectual ability among mistreated children. Our abused group had a larger proportion of children with higher than average ability than either the accident or the comparison group. (This is not congruent with the findings of Sandgrund, Gaines, and Green [1974]. Their neglected subjects and abused subjects scored significantly lower than their comparisons, although the abused children did not manifest the greatest impairment.) On the other hand, ten children out of the total fifty-nine had less-than-average ability. How far four of these ten deviated from the average cannot be established because of the indirect method of assessing their ability (that is, by means of records, not direct examination). We do know, though, that six of them, or 10 percent of the total sample, were in special classes for retarded children, implying a substantial degree of retardation.

This contrasts with the figure of 2 to 3 percent that is considered the percentage of mental retardation in the population at large (Farber, 1968). Thus, the proportion of mental retardation in this sample was at least three to five times as large as expected in the normal population.

The six children in special classes were distributed according to classification as follows: abuse, three; accident, two; and comparison, one. Four of these children (two abused and two accident) had significant neurological problems at Time Three, which helps explain their intellectual disability. The remaining two children had only minor neurological problems.

Achievement ratings across the sample, combining the untraumatized comparisons, were as follows:

	< *Average*	*Average*	> *Average*
Abuse	9	6	2
Accident	5	11	1
Combined comparisons	7	17	1

Although the proportion of less-than-average achievers was comparatively high in the abuse group, the only statistical group difference showed that the lower-certainty abuse group performed better than the high-certainty group (Fisher's Exact Probability, $p = .02$).

Three of the abused children whose achievement was low had poor neurological scores, as did one of the accident low achievers. Two other children, one accident and one comparison, also had poor neurological scores but were achieving at an average level.

The ratio of achievement to ability assesses how well a child can actually utilize his ability. Children whose school tests showed they were mentally retarded but who were achieving satisfactorily in special classes were categorized as equal in achievement and ability and were therefore rated as achieving up to expectation. Three retarded children were so rated. The ratio of achievement to ability across the sample, combining the untraumatized comparisons, was as follows:

	< *Average*	*Average*	> *Average*
Abuse	9	7	1
Accident	4	12	1
Combined comparisons	6	19	0

We had anticipated that the predicted emotional problems of the abused children would interfere with their intellectual performance. Whether or not emotional problems were the cause, half the abused children showed inadequate achievement compared with ability. Among the accident and combined comparison groups, the proportion of children showing a poor ratio of achievement to ability was much smaller: 26 percent and 24 percent, respectively. The differences between groups did not reach significance. It should be noted, however, that almost one-third of the total sample (including one-quarter of the untraumatized children) were performing poorly in the early years of school and this proportion undoubtedly will grow as educational tasks increase in difficulty. In fact, the teachers noted that several children, though now performing acceptably, were showing signs of declining.

Some children who were not achieving up to their ability had poor neurological scores (three of the nine abused, one of the four accident, and none of the six comparisons). Martin et al. (1974) have noted that neurological damage is by no means the only influence on the subsequent development of abused children. Moving frequently from one home to another can be another deleterious influence; the three abused children with poor ratios of achievement to ability and poor neurological scores also had histories of many changes in caretakers.

Richardson et al. (1973) found that severe malnourishment in infancy was associated with later inferior school performance in comparison with classmates. Although the children in our follow-up study had not been identified as severely malnourished, many of them were below the third percentile in weight when they were first known to us as infants. We therefore examined ability in school according to weight percentiles at Time One for all the traumatized children (abused and accident). (Similar measurements were not available for the comparison children, who were studied only at Time Three.) Children rated less than average in ability were combined with children who were not achieving up to their ability. This group was then compared as to weight percentiles at Time One with children of average or better than average ability whose school progress at Time Three was satisfactory. The latter group had weighed significantly more at Time One ($t_{32} =$ 2.62, $p < .02$).

Low weight as an infant may of course be only one of several negative influences during infancy that affect later cognitive functioning. Richardson (1972) has pointed out that poor physical growth is often accompanied by sparse stimulation, that is, few toys, limited reading material, little opportunity to go on trips. Although we did not formally assess the potential for stimulation of the environment affecting our sample, in many instances home observations revealed few books or pictures and little evidence of hobbies.

Social class is another major influence that must be considered with respect to the large proportion of the total sample that was achieving poorly in relation to ability. Bayley (1965) demonstrated that the developmental scores of healthy infants up to fifteen months of age are essentially the same, whatever their backgrounds. This is not the case for older children. Differences in test results based on social class are visible before the age of two and become more marked by school age (Ginsburg, 1972). Differences according to ethnicity as well as social class have been reported by Lesser, Fifer, and Clark (1965).

The majority of the children in our sample were members of lower-class families (classes IV and V), and half the group were blacks. The comparatively poor achievement of the abuse group in relation to ability may well stem largely from the mistreatment they experienced in infancy (and perhaps later), along with related factors such as poor health at Time One and malnutrition. But the poor ratio of achievement to ability shown by a large proportion of the entire group may be associated with the lower-class membership of most, which is combined with the minority status of many.

The highest possible overall score on the teacher questionnaire was 41 (actual range, 12–38). T-tests between the major groups showed no significant differences, although the seventeen abused children had lower scores than their accident matches. Significant differences did appear between the high-certainty subgroup and each of its comparison subgroups. The high-certainty subgroup had lower overall scores than the matched accident subgroup ($t_{22} = 2.67, p < .02$), the matched comparisons ($t_{22} = 3.15, p < .01$), and the low-certainty subgroup ($t_{15} = 3.39, p < .01$). The children in the high-certainty abuse subgroup were achieving at a poorer level than those in the lower-certainty group. Item analysis showed that the high-certainty abused children scored lower than the untraumatized ones on frustration tolerance ($x^2 = 4.69, p < .05$) and interest in school ($x^2 = 5.56, p < .02$), and had a lower attention span than their accident matches, but not at a significant level. Inability to withstand frustration and lack of interest in school are associated with the degree of investment in learning. At this stage of their school career, the effects on achievement have not been great, as shown by the nonsignificant results of comparisons of their achievement with those of the accident and untraumatized comparisons. Whether this will remain true is, of course, not known.

Clinical assessment of behavior. Control of aggression and degree of disturbance were evaluated. These assessments were based on summaries of all available material including mothers' comments, written reports of the follow-up clinicians, medical records, school records, teachers' questionnaires, and records from other agencies. Names and other identifying information were removed from all material.

Twenty-one children (36 percent) were judged as either variable or undercontrolled in aggression; thirty-three (56 percent), as overcontrolled; and only five (10 percent), as average. Ten children (17 percent) were assessed as moderately to severely disturbed; 24 (41 percent), as somewhat disturbed; and 25 (42 percent), as not disturbed or only slightly so. Comparisons between groups showed no differences for any of these ratings, but the number of individuals with one or more behavior problems was obviously high.

The pediatrician noted nervous mannerisms in many children, and these were the subject of inquiry on the teacher questionnaire. They included behaviors such as tics, biting of fingers or nails, and thumb sucking. The number of children mentioned as having any of these mannerisms was tallied and the groups compared. Curiously, the group with the fewest nervous mannerisms was the abuse group (29 percent). More than half the children in each of the other groups (accident and the combined accident and abuse comparisons) were listed as having at least one nervous mannerism. We surmised that the abused child might act out more and therefore have less need for this type of symptom. In line with this speculation, we would expect the abused children without nervous mannerisms to show a greater degree of one or more of the characteristics of impulsivity, aggression, or disturbance than abused children with nervous mannerisms. However, this conjecture did not prove true.

Three abused black boys impressed several clinicians as having a pronounced feminine identification. During the speech evaluation, one of these boys began to imitate a girl's voice. When the clinician commented on this, the child placed a towel over his head, saying that it was a wig, and continued to talk for the rest of the assessment period in a high falsetto voice. He said he enjoyed pretending to be a girl at home, and his foster mother later confirmed his enjoyment of feminine roles. Another boy was described by his foster mother as isolated from his peers and not interested in their activities. Instead, he enjoyed making clothes for his Barbie dolls, with which he played for hours on end, and he sometimes folded his arms high on his chest in imitation of breasts.

In another study it was found that sexual identification was at least outwardly established among 80 percent of the subjects by the time they were in first grade (Silver and Hagin, 1972). As the children in our sample were older, a larger percentage would be expected to have firm sexual identifications. Because of the gross nature of these three boys' behavior, we explored the records of the entire sample for evidence of similar problems among the other children. The examiners had commented on sexual problems of seven abused children, including the three already mentioned. One of the other four, a girl, was seen as showing marked homosexual trends. The difficulties of the remaining three were shown in behavior revealing a confusion of aggression and sexuality.

Of the forty-two children who were not abused, only seven revealed psychosexual problems. Five children had castration fears and the other two had uncertain sexual identification. All these problems appeared to be considerably milder than those of the abused group.

Thus, the follow-up examiners noted sexual problems among 41 percent of the abused children and 17 percent of the combined accident and comparison children. We had not anticipated differences of this nature among the groups; hence, these findings are not based on systematic procedures designed to elicit information concerning psychosexual development. The chance findings do appear to offer a fruitful lead for further investigation in other studies. We can, however, speculate about the feminine identification of the three abused boys. In each case the natural mother was thought to be the abuser, which suggests as explanation a form of identification with the aggressor. Another possible explanation is that all three children were responding to their perception of the world as a matriarchal society. Until recent years one frequently encountered such an analysis of family structure among blacks, although the validity of this formulation has been disputed (Baughman, 1971).

The Children in Substitute Homes

We had anticipated that the eight children who had been removed from their abusive environments and placed in foster or adoptive homes would function at a higher level than those who had remained in the natural abusive homes. However, once we had obtained the relevant records, we could see those children were at higher risk for poor performance. The results of the speech and language tests showed the children in substitute care to be statistically inferior to those in natural homes. (However, this may have been due to differences between the groups as to race and social class, a topic previously discussed.) They were not taller, nor did they weigh more. They had significantly smaller head circumferences ($t_{15} = 2.19$, $p < .05$), but the implications of this are uncertain. Otherwise our tests showed no significant differences between children living in substitute homes and any of the other groups (abused children living in natural homes and the matched accident and matched comparisons). The bald results of tests, however, do not convey the whole picture of these children. The three black boys mentioned as having such strong feminine identification were all in foster homes. One, according to his foster mother, seemed "to go into space" with the result that he would forget he was crossing a street, stop in the middle of traffic, and stare off into the distance. The foster mother feared he might be hit by a passing motorist, and there were also other situations in which this child endangered himself.

Among the reasons for the failure of the abused children in substitute care to surpass the rest of the abused children could be early neglect, poor health at Time One, and their history of placement prior to the final home. Reports from the placement agencies showed that four of these eight children had each lived in at least four different homes by the age of two years. One of these children had lived in four different homes before he was one year old, while still another had seven placements before the age of two. A fifth child was ultimately adopted at the age of forty-six months, but had frequently been abandoned, both by her mother and by strangers with whom the mother had left her. Finally, the mother disappeared for good.

The records of the children who were shuttled from here to there suggest that the placement agencies and the courts leaned over backwards to place the children with their natural mothers whenever the mothers wished to try again. There was little to suggest that any kind of intensive work had been done with these mothers as a condition for the return of their children. The result was that such returns, at least in relation to these specific children, did not work.

*A case example is a little boy whose placement career began at the age of three months. Following brief periods at institutions, foster homes, and stints with the natural mother, he ended up in a foster home where he stayed from the age of one until eight. The natural mother then went to court and requested his return home, a move that the court approved. Within six months he ran away from his natural mother and knocked on the door of the foster home where he had lived for so long. He was terror stricken and said that his natural mother had hurt him. On his buttocks he had a burn mark in the shape of a cross, an injury that had been inflicted by the natural mother, who was angry at the child's failure to respond lovingly. As the foster parents were no longer legally entitled to take care of the child, they took him to the police station; from there he went to a shelter where he stayed several months before final disposition in the same foster home as before. One can only imagine the terrible fears and conflicting feelings of loyalty that this child must have suffered. The foster mother reported that he had great difficulty going to sleep for several months after his return to her home. She sat up with him night after night trying to calm his nightmares.

Fortunately, the three remaining children of the eight in substitute care had better histories of placement. All had the good fortune to become settled in their new homes early in life without a good deal of moving.

Would the children in substitute homes have been better or worse off had they remained with the natural abusive families throughout these early years? Perhaps the multiple changes caused even greater psychological difficulties. The experiences of our children are very similar to those of children described by other investigators who have explored the question of substitute care. One researcher doubts the benefit of such placements because the children who are changed around so much develop into "extremely fragile" adults (Pavenstedt, 1971). On the other hand, the children in our study in substitute homes might have appeared even worse had they remained in homes where, in addition to abuse, neglectful care was apparently a commonplace. All the children who eventually were placed in substitute homes were classified at Time Two as high-certainty abuse, and all were neglected. The families of the high-certainty abuse subgroup compared unfavorably at Time One–Time Two with their matched accident subgroup families as to a range of variables, among them total stability (including stress and maternal health), total support, and the demographic characteristics of maternal education, marital status, and social class.

High-Certainty Abused Children Compared with Others

It is interesting to speculate why these children, with their histories of abuse plus chaotic and unpredictable living conditions, did not perform more poorly at Time Three than all the rest of the children in our sample. A possible answer to this speculation lies in the unexpected extent of pathology among the majority of the families in all groups, not just the abusive families. No one group stood out: most families appeared chaotic and poorly organized; many parents relied on drugs or alcohol; and most were living in circumstances of frequent violence. One child in the accident group was being reared by his single mother in the company of six older siblings. The mother, Miss O., was an obese diabetic woman who felt excluded from the community because of her repeated pregnancies. Perhaps as one response to the community attitude, she engaged in impulsive, destructive behavior. At one point she decided to get rid of all the old furniture in the house; she made a bonfire in the backyard on which she threw overstuffed chairs, old tables, rugs, and other household belongings. As the fire burned higher, she became more and more euphoric, finally pitching in not only the decrepit belongings but also those which the family depended on. She and her seven children then had to be taken in by neighbors because they lacked essential housekeeping articles.

Other forms of pathology were evident in the control group as well. The mother in one of these families reported an incident when she had lunged at the father with a butcher knife. He retaliated by breaking her arm and knocking out her front teeth. The same man had attacked his teen-age son with a knife because the boy had crossed the street against orders. By the time we evaluated the eight-year-old sibling, the parents had separated and scenes of violence were presumably reduced. But the mother had been on massive amounts of tranquilizers for six years without medical supervision; she spoke of herself as a zombie who scarcely knew what was going on.

One mother in the comparison group described a recent burglary of her home that had caused her to fire a gun at the unknown intruder. Another woman, who was in the accident group, talked of a neighborhood shoot-out when she and her children were forced to take refuge under beds and in stairwells (see the Wilson case in chapter 3). We had reports of fathers pushing mothers down stairs, women beating their children for minor infringements, and children attacking each other with knives and other deadly weapons. One little boy talked so convincingly of a prison that we wondered about his experience; we learned that his father had been incarcerated because he murdered another man.

We also found evidence suggesting unrecognized neglect. The medical records of one comparison child showed that his mother had brought him at the age of nine months to the emergency room of the local hospital with second-degree burns of the face, neck, and shoulders. She had been carrying him in the kitchen where a pot of soup was boiling on the stove. She said that the baby was whirling a toy pistol on a string that became entangled with the pot, causing it to spill over him. The glaring inconsistencies in this report were not picked up by the hospital staff. When the child was two years old, he was again seen in the emergency room, this time because he ingested a poisonous substance. A year later he was admitted after drinking wine. The accumulation of untoward and dangerous events in the life of this young child can hardly be explained without postulating negligence on the part of his caretakers.

The examiners' clinical impressions of the children were alike in disbelief that so many could appear so handicapped psychologically. Overall, the children had an air of depression, sadness, and anxiety. One girl in the accident group voiced suicidal wishes (see Appendix 3b). As part of the spontaneous stories told to the examiners, many children showed great concern that they might become the victims of attack. Most children of this age are involved with fantasies of witches, devils, and monsters that will harm them (Silver and Hagin, 1972), but the study children linked their fears of injury or mutilation to real persons. These persons might be parents, older children, or teachers. Six of the boys talked about being paddled in school.

Several children produced stories or fantasies that seemed to be associated with personal mistreatment. One abused child spent five minutes explaining and demonstrating with materials at hand just how a child might be tied with a lamp cord so he could be beaten. Some children found it impossible to invent a story with a happy ending. (This was an exercise given by the speech pathologist to produce material on which to assess expressive language.) One such child concluded his story with a happy ending by describing a motorcycle accident in which all the actors were killed.

A few of the children, while participating in the study procedures, demonstrated in their behavior a high degree of disturbance. One little girl, for example, threatened to jump out the fourth-floor window and actually ran toward it before she was stopped. Fortunately, we were prepared for some such behavior by this child as she had deliberately put her hand through a glass door while the interviewers were in the home. Still other children whose behavior in the laboratory was unremarkable were reported as showing problem behavior at home. A few weeks before we examined him, one of these children, an abused boy, had been discovered in the act of tying a rope around his younger sister's neck while she slept. This was not the first act of aggression against the sister, but it was by far the most serious.

The Families and the Children, Time Three: A Summary

We had not formulated hypotheses about the abusive and accident families at Time Three because eight of the twelve high-certainty children were living with substitute families by the time of the follow-up investigation. All groups of families (abusive, accident, comparison, as well as the foster/adoptive abuse subgroup) were remarkably similar as to demographic characteristics except that the foster/adoptive mothers were older than the other mothers and the accident families had lower incomes per person. In the overall stability index no differences appeared, but in one of the items, the mother's health, the natural abusive mothers were at a higher risk for child care than the foster/adoptive. At Time Three, the natural abusive mothers also had inferior support compared with that received by the substitute mothers. However, none of these findings were significant.

The fact that differences between abusive and accident families found at Time One–Time Two had disappeared or become attenuated by Time Three should not obscure the finding that the children who were placed in substitute homes had gained in familial stability; they undoubtedly were also beneficiaries of the higher support enjoyed by the substitute mothers. When the stability and support scores for their families at Time One were compared with scores on the same variables for their caretakers at Time Three, the differences were significant. No differences were seen in the kind of child care provided at Time Three by the various groups.

There were no significant differences between the groups concerning physical child care, the age at which mothers perceived their children had learned right from wrong, the number of different punishments they used, or the number of offenses leading to physical punishment, except in the case of the mothers of the high-certainty children, who perceived that their children had learned right from wrong at two years or more. Their matched accident mothers thought their children had learned at an earlier age. The failure to find group differences did not mean lack of variability among the mothers. The range of different punishments was great, as was the number of offenses that would be met by physical punishment. Behaviors that were inappropriate in relation to the offense were noted. Again, no differences appeared between the groups, but approximately half of every group showed what we judged to be inappropriate responses.

Our determination of maternal perception of the child, which entailed analyses of spontaneous remarks and elicited descriptions, showed that negative or neutral descriptions predominated in more than 50 percent of the entire sample, whatever the group classification. This suggests that half of the fifty-nine children were living in environments lacking in positive support, regardless of the presence or absence of abuse. Perhaps the use of remarks and replies to questions was too gross a method, for we failed to find the peculiarities that other investigators have identified with respect to parental attitudes toward their abused children. However, no other investigators have had the benefit of matched comparison groups.

The questionnaire developed for the follow-up study revealed that mothers of abused children saw their offspring as angrier than other children and mothers of accident children saw their offspring as more persevering and inclined to explore. By combining the latter findings with the higher motor activity over time of the accident children, we begin to see some related characteristics that merit further investigation as to the possibility of "accident-proneness."

We had hypothesized that the abused children would score lower than the nonabused in height and weight, language development, and intellectual functioning. However, few overall differences were found between the abused children, the accident children, and their respective comparison groups. The one subgroup that stood out to a degree consisted of the twelve high-certainty abused children. They were significantly taller and somewhat heavier than their matched comparison subgroup, a finding contrary to expectations. Their expressive language was significantly poorer than that found in either their matched accident or matched untraumatized subgroup. When language was explored according to substitute versus natural home, children in the substitute homes had lower ratings in expressive language, significantly lower ratings in articulation, and significantly more communication problems. Although the lower scores in language of the foster/ adoptive children (who formed the bulk of the high-certainty subgroup) may have been due partly to their early histories, race and socioeconomic class were thought to be equally important influences. However, except for their expressive language and head size, the foster/adoptive children appeared no different on our tests from the other groups, despite the gain in familial stability and support through their placement.

The high-certainty abused children were inferior to the lower-certainty group in achievement in school. A greater proportion of abused children had a poor ratio of achievement to ability, but no significant differences appeared between any of the groups as to this ratio. The teacher questionnaires picked out the children in the high-certainty abuse subgroup as having significantly less interest in school and lower frustration tolerance than their matched comparisons. The overall scores for the teacher questionnaire were significantly lower for the high-certainty subgroup than for any of its comparison subgroups.

We had also hypothesized that the abused children would score higher than the nonabused in number of interim illnesses and injuries and in impulsivity and aggression, but lower in empathy. In relation to illnesses and injuries, only the accident children had a statistically greater number, and this was in relation to their untraumatized comparisons. A few differences were found as to the increase in aggression and impulsivity through the role-play stories, all of which indicated that the abuse group showed a greater increase in the exhibition of these traits than the accident group. These results merit exploration, but may be chance findings. The only difference in empathy was sex-based. Although we had not been searching for psychosexual problems, we found many more among the abuse group than in all the rest of the sample. It may prove worthwhile to explore this further in other studies. Our hypothesis that the abused children would score lower on self-concept was not corroborated. As in other procedures, there was a wide variation in results, but high and low scores were evenly distributed across all the groups.

The results of this follow-up study indicate that only a few of our hypotheses were accurate, and most of the significant findings pertained not to the major groups but to the smaller subgroups. Where there were differences between the abused and another group, they were always in relation to *one* of the other groups, not both. This was a culmination of a process that we had observed since Time Two, the end of the Infant Accident Study. As will be recalled, the abused and accident children were very similar as to conditions at birth and the later injuries that brought them to our study. At Time One, only a few short months after birth, the abused children had significantly more health problems than the accident children, but there were few other differences between the two groups. By Time Two even those differences had begun to disappear; the children appeared alike in more ways, that is, anthropometric measures and mood. The abused children, however, still had more health problems. By Time Three the two traumatized groups had become increasingly alike and, what is more, could not be distinguished from their comparison groups. At the end of Time Three we summed all the current problems for each child that could have been detected by our procedures and found nineteen categories. We used the mean score for number of problems to compare the groups. The abuse group had an average score of 6.24 and its comparison group an average of 4.53; the accident group had an average score of 5.18 and its comparison group had 4.71. A t-test revealed no significant differences between the groups. Figure 1 shows according to general category the extent of the difficulties with which all children were struggling.

Although the groups of children became more alike, the children within each group showed wide variations on each individual test. For example, the scores for expressive language ran from excellent to very poor. The same was true for almost every other procedure in our study. It appeared that factors other than abuse might account for the observed variations among the individual children.

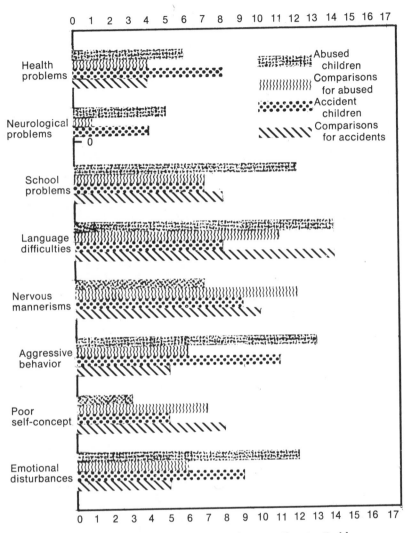

FIGURE 1. Number of Children in Each Group Showing Problems

In an attempt to discover some of these factors, we made a final assessment of the data, a procedure not planned in the original follow-up study. This assessment disregarded group classification (abuse, accident, or comparison) and concentrated instead on identifying possible independent variables that might be associated with nine selected child characteristics as measured in this study. These characteristics, called child-outcome variables, were expressive language, intellectual ability in school, school achievement, achievement in relation to ability, separation problems, nervous mannerisms, overcontrol of aggression, undercontrol of aggression, and degree of disturbance. Among the independent or predictor variables were items related to the family (for example, education of the mother, stability, maternal perception of the child, and, of course, abuse) and items related to the child (for example, number of operations and hospitalizations and interest in school). The predictor variables were based on data available for the total sample: that is, pregnancy and birth data and information from the time of the follow-up study. Predictor and outcome variables did not overlap. This procedure was developed by Lachin (1973).[20]

Four of the nine child-outcome variables produced either ambiguous results or three or more predictors whose patterns were too complex to be useful with respect to this small sample. The remaining child outcomes were intellectual ability, school achievement, separation problems, undercontrol of aggression, and degree of disturbance.

As the child-outcome and predictor variable analysis was peripheral to the main follow-up study, only an overview of the results and comments as to their relevance for this study of abuse are given here. The predictor variables that the Lachin program selected in relation to each child outcome were logical ones; for example, average or better intellectual ability in the child was shown to be related to better than average maternal education (high school or more) and low frequency of punishment, both variables working together. The selected predictor variables were also supported by other results of this study. For example, overcontrolled aggression or average control of aggression in the child was associated with low role-play aggression in the dramatic story procedure (as well as better than average maternal education). Finally, the predictor variables were supported by the findings of other research; for example, average or better school achievement was associated with high interest in school. For each child outcome, the percentage of the sample correctly selected by a combination of predictor variables ranged from 45 percent to 95 percent. However, since this procedure was largely an expedition of speculation, the validity of the chosen predictors in relation to each outcome would need to be tested by analyzing a different sample of children.

The other result of note is the absence of abuse as a predictor variable for any of the final five child outcomes: no relationship appeared between abuse and any of the child-outcome variables. This finding supports the results of the other procedures described in this book, namely, that few differences emerged between the groups.

Completing the Circle

When the follow-up study was completed, we were at a loss to explain the lack of significant results differentiating between the abused, accident, and comparison groups or any of the subgroups. Across the board there were very few differences between the groups, and these were relatively minor. The follow-up staff was astonished and disbelieving. It then turned out that several of the examiners had kept a private tally showing their opinions of the classifications of each child. In no case had these tallies been correct any more often than would be true of selections made purely by chance. In addition, the clinicians' opinions had differed for individual children, showing that their combined judgments could not effectively differentiate the groups.

At first we felt something must have been wrong with the study, and we reviewed the entire design and methodology. Obviously, the absence of differences could have resulted from errors in judgment at Time One concerning which child was abused and which accidentally injured.[21] At Time One few data were available on which to make a solid diagnosis, and judgments then were bound to be probabilistic. Furthermore, there is an overlap between abuse and accident in that abused children can have genuine accidents, with the result that our judgment could have been confounded. As noted before, infants who are well developed and well nourished and who have either no injury or very slight ones are difficult to diagnose as abused, especially if the family is neatly dressed and articulate.

It will be recalled that five families who were classified in the accident category at Time One were reclassified as abusive at Time Two because of observations by the staff and reports of family members concerning extreme methods of punishment. For example, the research social worker was present when Mrs. T. (one of the lower-certainty mothers) placed a basket of apples in a passageway where the child would be attracted to them. When he touched them, the mother administered a fierce beating because she had told him previously that he must not touch. Mrs. T. explained to the social worker that she believed one must teach a child to resist temptation and punish him when he failed. It was hard to believe she was speaking of a child not yet two years old. In another context Mrs. T. quoted the following line to justify her frequent corporal punishment of her son: "Spare not the rod, for the blueness of the wound will bring sweetness to the heart." Eight years later, in the follow-up study, the same mother spoke of herself as abusive and described other exceedingly aggressive acts against both the index child and his older sibling. She thus confirmed the judgment of abuse that we had made at the conclusion of the Infant Accident Study.

It is also possible that some other children who were actually abused were misclassified as accident at both Time One and Time Two, and others who had had valid accidents were misjudged as abused. However, we guarded against errors in classification by collecting data over a one-year period and by utilizing a range of data-collecting procedures.

Another source of possible error was the selection of comparison cases for the follow-up. One of the criteria for selecting these cases was the absence of reported abuse. The fact that Child Welfare Services had no record of abuse need not mean that it did not occur; abuse could have been part of the family child-rearing practices but might never have resulted in an injury severe enough to warrant medical attention. Similarly, abused injured children might not have been reported as abused; we know that many physicians have a low index of suspicion when a parent reports accidents and there was no mandatory reporting law in Pennsylvania during the early part of our study. Another reason for the lack of difference between the traumatized children and the comparison children is the possibility that some process of self-selection was operating with respect to the comparison children whom we examined. The Barry case (see chapter 3) is an example of a mother's hidden agenda to get help for a child's problem. If many comparison mothers had been similarly motivated to join the study, the comparison group would have been skewed toward pathology.

We made many efforts to minimize these possible errors. Besides exercising all the caution possible in making the original judgments, in the follow-up study we gathered data in a variety of situations. A child who did not do well in one might have shown up better in another. We also engaged a range of professionals to do the examinations and ensured that they performed their functions without any knowledge of the child's classification. In two instances, however, the data-collecting procedures might not have been sufficiently revealing. The administration of a battery of psychological tests probably would have been more helpful than a review of school records. (Most helpful, of course, would have been a combination of the two procedures.) Likewise, the groups might have been differentiated better through the use of a structured psychiatric interview for each child rather than review of the records by three professionals. We do not believe, however, that these two changes in methodology would have altered our findings in any major way. The number of data-gathering procedures, the range of professionals utilized as examiners, and the facts of the family histories serve to validate our conclusions.

After reviewing our design and methodology, we examined several other possible interpretations of our results. All but one of the children in the sample lived in the Greater Pittsburgh Metropolitan Area, all were known to a hospital, and the majority were identified with the lower classes. (1) Are children living in Pittsburgh subjected to poorer methods of child-rearing than their peers in other communities? Although this hypothesis appears unlikely, it cannot be disputed without studies of other children matched on the relevant variables and reared in other locations. (2) Since all the children came from hospital populations, did all the parents utilize exceptionally harsh child-rearing methods? If social class is held constant, there is no valid reason to postulate a difference between hospital clients and nonhospital clients as to the use of aggression in child-rearing. (3) Did treatment in a hospital at an early age somehow permanently affect these children? The children had a broad range of injuries — from none to very severe. Some spent half an hour as outpatients, others up to several weeks as inpatients. It is hard to imagine that such differing experiences could have exerted a uniform effect years later. (4) Could the entire sample (not just the abused children) have been subjected repeatedly to uncontrolled aggression at the hands of their caretakers, who used such methods because of their lower-class membership? No conclusive data presently exist to confirm such an explanation.

Thus, in our review of design, methodology, and possible interpretations, we saw no major flaws that would have discounted our results. It was impossible to avoid the conclusion that abuse as one method of deviant child care did not appear to make a significant difference, at least in the population under study. In addition, our clinical observations had shown unanticipated pathology among most families in all the groups and evidence of considerable psychological damage in many of the children. What could be the common factor contributing to these widespread difficulties? We believe this factor is membership of the majority in the lower social classes, which connotes poverty and all its well-known companions: poor education, menial jobs, inadequate housing, undernutrition, poor health, and environmental violence (Lampkin, 1971). This will be discussed more fully in the concluding chapter. Validation of the results of our follow-up study, however, awaits similar investigations of children living in other communities and from a range of social classes. The use of matched comparison groups to evaluate the outcome for abused children does offer a means to correct conclusions based on the study of abused children alone.

Although some of the children were not of the lower social classes (IV and V), they nevertheless appeared like the others. Two possible explanations come to mind: some of those with higher socioeconomic status at Time Three (classes II and III) had been living in more straitened circumstances at Time One and Time Two, and early experiences are considered crucial for child development. The second reason is that social status is only a crude indicator of the quality of the home. As we have seen, the relative support and stability of the families at Time Three were essentially the same, and this may indicate an equally poor cognitive and nurturing environment. "[Deprivation] is more closely related to social and emotional disorders within the family than to economic status, and, in fact, has been described in families of relatively high socio-economic position" (Patton and Gardner, 1963, p. 16).

Three Case Studies

Carol Custer: An Abused Child

Carol Custer, a white female infant, was nine months old when she was seen in the radiology department of Children's Hospital of Pittsburgh on the referral of the family's private physician. Mrs. Custer gave a history of persistent weakness in both the child's feet, which had led to a prescription for special exercises from a local orthopedic clinic. Recently, the left knee had become red, swollen, and hard between the ankle and the knee. The baby refused to bear weight on it. She was taken to the emergency room of a local hospital where x-rays were made of both legs and infection was diagnosed. After treatment with antibiotics gave no relief, the family physician asked for a diagnostic opinion from Children's Hospital.

Various items in the history were of interest with reference to abuse or accident. When Carol was three months old, the family was preparing to go on a trip. In some unexplained fashion, the baby's head was bumped and x-rays revealed a linear fracture of the skull. When Carol was about eight months old, she was left with friends of her mother. Although surrounded by pillows on the couch, somehow she wiggled to the edge and pushed herself off. When her mother returned fifteen minutes later, she found the baby whimpering on the floor. No medical attention was sought as Mrs. Custer saw no signs of injury.

At the Children's Hospital a skeletal x-ray revealed several fractures incurred at different times. The old fracture of the skull appeared, as did relatively new fractures of both legs affecting the long bone near the ankle. In addition, two ribs were fractured and the baby had two bruises, one on her chest and one on her face.

According to the radiologist, the leg injuries could not have resulted from a fall; instead, some kind of twisting force would have been required. However, Mrs. Custer could think of no possible explanation and seemed unconcerned about the baby's condition.

The family's physician was very hesitant to do anything about the apparently abusive injuries. There was then no reporting law in Pennsylvania, and consequently the practitioner had more leeway than would be true at the present time. He did agree to permit the family to enter the Infant Accident Study and encouraged them to participate.

The research interviewer arranged to see Mrs. Custer at home. The small rented house was adequately but sparsely furnished. Little attention had been paid to arrangement, color, or shape, and the interviewer's impression was one of flat dullness.

Except for an air of discontent and disgruntlement, Mrs. Custer was an attractive woman of twenty-one with heavy, smooth, black hair and a very fair complexion. She answered direct questions as briefly as possible and without elaboration. She was not openly hostile but had little interest in the interview or the reasons for it and could think of no explanation for Carol's injuries. The radiologist had told her that the fractures of the leg had to be incurred through twisting. She accepted this apathetically and was not stirred to search for the cause. Her attitude was puzzling; most parents deny such a diagnosis, become angry, or try vigorously to think of other possible explanations.

Mrs. Custer had a high-school education and was pregnant with Carol when she got married. In the fourteen months since her marriage, she and her husband had separated four times. According to the mother, the root of the problem was Mr. Custer's drinking. Because of her distress over the marital situation, Mrs. Custer had had to go on tranquilizers. This led to difficulty in caring for the baby; consequently, the maternal grandmother took charge of the child as needed. At the time of the initial home interview, the couple were separated for the fourth time, and Mrs. Custer and Carol were living alone. Mrs. Custer helped out intermittently as a clerk in a neighborhood newsstand while the grandmother cared for Carol.

Mrs. Custer referred several times to her husband's marked immaturity. He was twenty years old, a high-school graduate, and worked on a local assembly line. His work hours changed every week, a schedule that Mrs. Custer said made living arrangements very difficult. He still thought of "the boys" as his family, spending most of his leisure time with them. The group was currently enthusiastic about stock-car racing, and Mr. Custer was buying a car to modify for this purpose, despite family needs that Mrs. Custer thought should come first. It had always been difficult for her to plan finances as she never knew how much money he would give her. And just now, during his absence from home, he was doling out even less. Friends had told Mrs. Custer that her husband would eventually settle down and that they would go on to a happy life together. She felt little hope that this might happen.

Religious activities were one of Mrs. Custer's main interests. She belonged to a fundamentalist sect whose minister was able to provide twenty-four-hour telephone counseling. Various other sources of emotional support were also available to her. For example, she said that she liked her neighborhood, could call on her landlord for help when needed, and frequently talked about her worries with her husband's parents or her own father. Curiously, she did not mention her mother in this context.

Later, in a separate interview, the maternal grandmother spontaneously reported that Mrs. Custer often failed to feed the baby and found little enjoyment in the child, leaving her to her own amusement for hours at a time. The grandmother disapproved of this strongly. One wonders why she did not offer Mrs. Custer greater warmth and sympathy; at the same time she was investing many hours at inconvenient times to care for the baby, thus enabling Mrs. Custer to earn a little needed money. Our attempts to see Mr. Custer were unsuccessful, largely because his wife clearly opposed it.

When Mrs. Custer brought the baby to the outpatient department for the initial Infant Accident Study evaluation, we found the pregnancy had been greatly desired and the mother had been pleased to have a girl. The pregnancy was uneventful and gestation was forty weeks. Labor was normal, but the baby was delivered by breech presentation. Carol's birth measurements were within normal range (weight six pounds and length twenty-one inches). The only reported disability or illness was a chronic tendency for the feet to turn in. The Infant Accident Study pediatrician found that the baby was in the fortieth percentile for weight, twenty-fifth for height, and that her head and chest were within normal parameters. She still had evidences of bruises over the right eye and on the right chest; neither of these could be explained.

Results on the infant tests showed that Carol was slower than normal in motor development, was slightly advanced in mental development, and had normal language ability for her age. The doctor noted signs of mild spasticity in the lower extremities shown by hypotonicity, hyperreflexia, and delayed motor development. The baby impressed the examiners as being a bit stolid (not inclined to respond easily), but within normal expectations.

In reviewing the initial data, the staff saw three alternative explanations for Carol's injuries: birth trauma, accident, or abuse. Careful perusal of the birth records and consultation with the family doctor produced no evidence of damage to the legs during delivery, despite the breech presentation. Absence of known evidence, however, does not establish the absence of injury but only the fact that none was noticed. A more decisive reason for discounting birth trauma as the source of the fractures was the x-ray film, which indicated the presence of bone lesions at nine months of age. Typically, by this age bone damage stemming from delivery would have mended and thus would not be visible on film.

"Normal" accidents were another possibility, but several lines of reasoning made this seem implausible. First, there was no history of accident for either the fracture of the skull or the bruises of the face and chest. Second, the fall from the couch described by Mrs. Custer did not account for the nature of the fractures of the legs.

Third, an infant who has this number of injuries is considered to be receiving grossly inadequate care because the relatively immobile baby is as yet incapable of propelling itself into dangerous situations by climbing, jumping, and exploring. This would have been especially true of Carol, whose motor development was slow.

The final possible explanation was abuse. This diagnosis was chosen not only through exclusion of birth trauma and accident but also because of findings of family difficulties that are known to place the young child in jeopardy. The parents were undergoing marked stress, as seen in their ambivalence toward a forced marriage, Mr. Custer's failure to become involved with his wife and child, and Mrs. Custer's apathy and implicit depression, feelings of aloneness, and her refuge in drugs and resulting failure to attend to the baby's basic needs.

Mrs. Custer brought Carol for a second evaluation one year later. By this time, Carol's motor development had slowed perceptibly and was now significantly below normal. Both language and mental development were average. Measures of temperament showed some changes: activity, which was measured initially as high, was measured now as low. Mood, initially measured as negative, had by now become positive. Of all the mothers seen at this point in the study, Mrs. Custer impressed the examiners as one of the harshest and most impatient with her child. She made many demands on the little girl and handled her roughly throughout the examination, particularly while dressing her.

At this time the parents were again separated, and Mrs. Custer exhibited much the same apathy and lack of interest as before, but the grandmother appeared very involved and interested in the care of the child.

At the conclusion of the Infant Accident Study, the staff found no reason to question the initial diagnosis of abuse. There was still no adequate explanation of the infantile injuries; in addition the mother's handling of the baby while being observed gave weight to the opinion that her relationship with the child was colored by hostility and tension.

The staff of the Infant Accident Study firmly believed that this family needed immediate help to avoid further strain and to lessen the chance of additional abuse. Mrs. Custer, however, refused to consider discussing her situation with anyone except her minister, whom she saw as providing all the help she wanted. We considered Mrs. Custer's attitude another sign of her feelings of hopelessness but, of course, we had to accept her decision.

When the family was seen about eight years later, the parents were again living together, and they had their own house. A second child, Ricky, had been born, and he was three. An undertone of lack of interest and engagement could still be felt. This came out particularly as Mrs. Custer described her usual activities. She had nothing that she thoroughly enjoyed or thoroughly disliked. She felt the marital problems had decreased as she and her husband had become more mature. At the same time she made critical comments about Mr. Custer's failure to do much around the house. His help was confined to occasionally mowing the lawn or carrying out garbage. He loved the children but spent almost no time with them and never did necessary chores such as taking them for doctor's appointments.

In response to a standard question concerning recent stresses in the family, Mrs. Custer could think of none. True, Mr. Custer had been laid off from work for four months. She had dreaded this possibility, but when it had occurred the family was able to keep its debts manageable, and both sets of grandparents aided financially.

Mr. Custer had been in two serious accidents. The racing car discussed in the first interview had been the means of one, making necessary a prolonged hospital stay. His jaw had been broken in several places, all his teeth knocked out, and various internal injuries suffered. Approximately a year before this accident, Mr. Custer had totally wrecked his automobile but without grave injuries to himself. Mrs. Custer thought this accident was not surprising in view of the number of speeding tickets he had received.

Mrs. Custer was still an active churchgoer and still relied on the minister as someone to talk to. She felt neither set of grandparents was helpful and remarked, "I don't believe in involving others in intimate family problems." She did allow them to baby-sit on occasion. Ricky, the younger child, was considered the "dummy" of the family, and Mrs. Custer criticized him in various ways. She spoke of her difficulties in keeping the two children from fighting. They slept together in one bed and Ricky was in the habit of waking Carol around five in the morning by pushing her off the bed. Despite the quarrels that this engendered and despite Mrs. Custer's distress, she had made no decisive move to correct the situation.

Mrs. Custer described Carol in lackluster terms that conveyed almost no picture of the child, either positive or negative. Carol was "about average," obedient, not interested in trying new things, a member of no children's groups. She was not allowed to make noise around the house or have her friends over because her father, now steadily on night shift, had to sleep in the daytime.

Mrs. Custer stated that Carol knew right from wrong by the age of one and a half. Now, whenever Carol deliberately did something wrong, Mrs. Custer used one of three punishments: whipping, teasing, or keeping the child inside the house, for staying inside "drives her [Carol] nuts." Mr. Custer's methods of punishment were modeled on the concept of "an eye for an eye." When Carol accidentally damaged a neighbor child's toy rocket, Mr. Custer took a hammer and destroyed a similar toy belonging to Carol.

One of the standard interview items was to ask what the mother wished to do for the child, either now or in the future. Mrs. Custer answered very simply, "Nothing." She explained this by stating that she did not believe in setting goals for children; they should develop at their own speed.

Carol's sessions with the examiners were pleasing all the way around. She was seen as a well-developed, alert, and sensitive young girl. She apparently enjoyed the sessions and did well in the different situations. It was only when we began examining her school record that we could see any sign of difficulty that might be related to this child's early experience with severe, unexplained injuries. Although not a brilliant girl, Carol had adequate intellectual endowment to do the required schoolwork. Her difficulty took the form of very uneven work despite her best efforts.

When we investigated possible supportive forces in Carol's life, we found that the grandmother had continued to play such a role, taking Carol for weekends, seeing that she got various advantages, and providing some of the steadiness that the parents lacked.

In looking back over the history, one gets the impression that the family had indeed matured and was doing better as a family group at Time Three than at Time One or Time Two. After much indecisiveness as to whether they wanted to live together, the parents had finally decided that they would try to make a go of it, and had found some way of living together in a little more peace.

At this time, however, there was still no satisfactory explanation for the extensive injuries that Carol had suffered as an infant. One wonders not only about the early stresses in the family, but at the significance of Mr. Custer's two serious accidents within a short perod of time. Were these merely a coincidence? Or were they signs of impulsivity that had to be acted out in some way and might have come to the fore in relation to the frustrations so prominent in the early years of the marriage?

During our follow-up procedures, Carol displayed few of the sequelae thought to be associated with mistreatment. No sign of difficulty was seen in her use of language, her story production, or her play. She was outgoing, interested, and able to relate to the clinicians. The one area in which performance and ability were out of balance was in the schoolroom, where it was increasingly necessary to manipulate and master abstract concepts, and this Carol could do only sporadically. It is possible that abused children think concretely and have trouble dealing with conceptual material. Nonetheless, there is no way to plot a direct association between this difficulty and Carol's early experience.

We might speculate concerning the reason for Carol's relative intactness at age eight. One factor could be the improved stability of the family, shown by the lessening of separations and the purchase of a house. Although Mrs. Custer still appeared uninvolved and apathetic, she too had improved to the extent that she no longer relied on tranquilizers. Mrs. Custer now appeared to have another object for the negativism previously directed toward

Carol, and this was the new brother. A much more positive force for Carol was the availability of a loving, caring grandmother who had tended to her infant granddaughter although unable to offer emotional support to her own daughter. She had maintained her interest in Carol and had demonstrated this by concrete activities throughout the period covered by our follow-up. A stable grandparent who can be part of a child's daily life is of great importance for any young person. Such a figure is immensely more important for the child whose immediate environment is fraught with the ambiguities and shadows of Carol's infancy.

Finally, Carol herself could well have had innate strengths that maintained a comparatively healthy rate of development in spite of difficulties in the family. Sobel (1973) has observed that traumatic histories are common among the general population as well as the psychiatric patient group. "What went right?" remains an intriguing and, so far, mystifying question.

Johnny Wilson: A Case of Accident

Johnny, a nine-and-a-half-month-old black male, was brought to the emergency room of Children's Hospital because of a laceration of the ring finger of the left hand. His mother had left him in a stroller in the care of an older sibling who apparently pushed or leaned on the stroller, causing Johnny's hand to be caught in one of the moving parts. Several sutures were required to close the wound, which healed satisfactorily.

Johnny's mother was agreeable to entering the Infant Accident Study and readily arranged an appointment for a home interview. The small second-floor apartment was in a run-down black ghetto of the central city; nevertheless, the quarters appeared neat and well cared for. Ms. Wilson, a twenty-five-year-old single woman, made her home with an unmarried sister, aged thirty-three. Both women received welfare assistance. Johnny was the youngest of three children and had a three-year-old sister and a five-year-old brother, neither of them fathered by Johnny's father.

Ms. Wilson elaborated on the accident to Johnny's finger. She had been watching television in the living room with her three children when the doorbell rang. She had lifted Johnny into the stroller, then had gone downstairs to see who was there. When she returned, Johnny's finger was spurting blood and the older child, crying and confused, could scarcely describe what had happened. Ms. Wilson immediately called a jitney (a form of taxi) and took Johnny to the hospital.

The interviewer's impression of Ms. Wilson was one of being "too tired." She appeared unable to initiate any activity but instead seemed to respond to the strongest of the currents passing her, whatever it might be. She was friendly and pleasant, not particularly intelligent, and said she had finished tenth grade.

In passing, Ms. Wilson mentioned that she could have used the help of Johnny's father at the time of the accident, if only he had been present. She had not seen him for some months and actually knew very little about him. For example, although she knew his age (twenty-nine), she did not know the date of his birth, his current address, or where he had attended school. She could recall that he was in construction work. Reading between the lines, one would assume that this was a temporary liaison with little basis in shared experiences or interests.

The pregnancy with Johnny had been an anxious time for Ms. Wilson. She was living alone, had two young children, then aged two and four, and had no adult to depend on. In the fifth month of pregnancy, she had contracted pneumonia. Although sick for two weeks, she had received only outpatient treatment. When the time of delivery approached, Ms. Wilson began to suffer labor pains that went on for two weeks. She was finally admitted to the hospital where medication was given to induce active labor. When this was ineffective, she was discharged with instructions to return "when labor really began."

Two days later she did return, this time in active labor. A breech presentation, Johnny was born after only two hours. Birth weight was six pounds, nine ounces; length was twenty-one inches. Both measurements were well within the normal range for a full-term baby. There were no neonatal problems.

When Johnny came for pediatric examination as part of the Infant Accident Study, we learned that he had had a series of contacts with Children's Hospital. In his short life of nine-and-a-half months, he had been seen on nine occasions by hospital staff, including one admission for urinary-tract infection. During this hospitalization, which lasted ten days, Ms. Wilson had visited him seven times, a formidable accomplishment for a mother with two other small children and no husband. Johnny's other visits to the hospital were caused by upper-respiratory infections and infections of the ears, none serious in itself but cause for concern in an infant of such tender age. Despite these negative experiences, Johnny was seen as an alert, bright, active child, well developed and well nourished, and average in all phases of development. His mother described him as very happy, spoiled, and a child who liked to fight.

Ms. Wilson had not been taking Johnny for routine well-child care. She was aware of the need for such attention and said she expected to take him the following month. Because of this failure, Johnny had had no immunizations and therefore was unnecessarily vulnerable to early childhood diseases.

Ms. Wilson herself appeared to be in good health although quite overweight. She requested help in making arrangements for an appointment in the family-planning clinic. When Ms. Wilson brought Johnny for his final pediatric examination as part of the Infant Accident Study, she had in tow a three-month-old daughter. She had gone to the family-planning clinic but had found that she was already pregnant, a fact that made her feel terrible, as she wanted no more children.

Johnny's motor and mental development could not be measured directly because of his exceedingly negative and uncooperative attitude. Ms. Wilson reported that he had walked alone at ten months, indicating slightly advanced motor development. She also said Johnny was beginning to combine words into short sentences, an ability that placed him in the normal range of intelligence. However, he would not say a word in the presence of the examiner. He was still getting a bottle at the age of twenty-two months, and often fought his younger sister in an attempt to take hers. Indeed, Ms. Wilson said he fought all the time: as soon as an uncle or an aunt walked into the room, he would hurl pop bottles or ashtrays at the individual. We were concerned at these reports, not only because of Johnny's behavior, but also because of Ms. Wilson's clear inability to control him — in fact, her failure to perceive the need for control.

In being allowed to throw the objects at his relatives, Johnny was being taught to act as he pleased. An associated maternal behavior was observed during the teaching-task assignment, part of the final evaluative procedure of the Infant Accident Study, in which the mother was to teach the child how to build a simple figure with blocks of graduated sizes. When Johnny did not immediately react to the blocks, Ms. Wilson, instead of trying to motivate him, began making excuses for him: "He's too sleepy, too tired." "Please take the blocks away; he can't do it." Thus, there were two examples of the child's behaving as he wished coupled with the absence of maternal expectations or goals to guide his conduct.

Johnny was very small physically at this time and was described by the pediatrician as a "failure-to-thrive" baby. His weight was the same as the fiftieth percentile for a child of eleven months, and his height was the same as the fiftieth percentile for seventeen months. The pediatrician, worried at the slowing trend in physical growth, suspected iron-deficiency anemia. A complete blood count was ordered, supplementary iron was prescribed, and Ms. Wilson was urged to bring Johnny to the hospital outpatient clinic for continuing care. However, she still had not taken Johnny to the well-baby clinic although it had been recommended one year before, and Johnny still had had no immunizations. We suspected that the mother would not bestir herself to get the clinic care either, so several extra home visits were planned by the social worker in an attempt to motivate her.

During the interval between the final pediatric examination of the Infant Accident Study and the first planned home visit, Ms. Wilson telephoned in a panic. Johnny had swallowed rat poison; what should she do? She was advised to administer an emetic, then to bring him to the Poison Control Center of the hospital. According to the medical chart, Johnny was seen later that day in Poison Control where it was learned that he had vomited following the emetic. He appeared none the worse for his experience and was referred to the outpatient clinic after being examined. Ingestion of poison, of course, suggests some deficiency in child care, another reason for additional attention to the family.

When the social worker went to the home for the planned visit, she found that Ms. Wilson had forgotten the appointment. Nevertheless, she was cordial and hospitable. The living room contained only three pieces of furniture, all of them battered and dirty. In contrast, the family members were neatly dressed and clean.

Ms. Wilson had now concluded that Johnny had not swallowed the rat poison. She remembered wedging the poison container between a chair and the wall, where Johnny could not reach it. It had become dislodged, and when she found it, she had assumed that Johnny must have eaten some of it. She had not taken him to the clinic as directed by both the emergency-room physician and the Infant Accident Study pediatrician because she did not have the bus fare.

She described Johnny as totally changed. He no longer threw objects, nor did he fight. The social worker attempted to draw her into further discussion of Johnny, but Ms. Wilson was unconcerned about his drop in weight and denied having any problem with either his care or his behavior. One reason for her lack of concern about her son might have been her anxiety in relation to her own health. She had recently learned that her blood pressure was dangerously high and she was required to go on a very rigid low-calorie diet. However, the prescribed appetite depressant had produced adverse side effects and she no longer took it. Ms. Wilson's mother had died at age forty-two from complications of high blood pressure and both her sister and an older brother had the same problem. She was clearly very frightened and was doing her best to follow medical directions.

The social worker had two additional interviews with Ms. Wilson, who remained little concerned about Johnny. She did, however, have concrete needs that the worker addressed, for example, better living quarters, toys for Christmas, and difficulty with bills. Ms. Wilson mentioned rather wistfully that she had nobody to talk to. The only time she could get away from her children was while waiting to see the doctor at Children's Hospital.

In our final evaluation conference, the Infant Accident Study staff voiced two concerns about the Wilson family: what was happening in the mother-baby relationship and Ms. Wilson's need for continued support, especially in view of her physical condition. We made strong recommendations to both Ms. Wilson and the Children's Hospital staff that ongoing efforts be made in both areas.

Eight years later we again saw Ms. Wilson, this time for the follow-up of Johnny, now almost ten. She was much heavier than before and was again on a rigid diet. She told the interviewer that high blood pressure had been diagnosed for the first time just three months before. She also described herself as nervous, especially at night, and complained of frequent headaches that sometimes lasted all day. The previous year she had broken out in hives, which made her most uncomfortable and required several kinds of medication.

At this time Ms. Wilson talked glowingly of Johnny's father, who she said had died six years earlier following an overdose of heroin. It had been very hard for her to get along without him. However, she did have three sisters and two brothers to whom she could talk, and she regarded them as solid supports. She was no longer sharing the apartment with her sister. She was still receiving welfare and had many financial limitations.

Ms. Wilson described Johnny as an easygoing boy who had lots of fun and enjoyed numerous sports, for example, swimming, football, and basketball. He was the most enjoyable of all her children. In the summer he went to a day camp, and during the school year he attended a boys' club. He was in fourth grade and regarded school as all right but not exciting. Often he talked too much and was made to stand in the coatroom. This year Johnny had missed twenty-three days of school because of colds.

Ms. Wilson said she "fell apart" when any of her children did something to endanger himself or others. Even more upsetting to her were dangerous events in the neighborhood over which she had no control. A few evenings before, the neighbors began shooting at each other while children were playing between them. Ms. Wilson was ultimately able to corral her children into the house, where she called the police. This time nobody was hurt, but once before, in similar circumstances, a neighbor child had received a superficial bullet wound.

Review of the medical records for the interim period from the conclusion of the Infant Accident Study to the follow-up study showed that Johnny had continued to have frequent contacts with Children's Hospital but at a lower rate than as an infant. For example, he had been seen seven times in 1968, four times each in 1969 and 1970, then once or twice in each of the succeeding years. Most of his complaints involved ear infections or upper-respiratory infections. He also began to have vague abdominal pains and headaches suggestive of psychosomatic symptoms. A few months before he was seen in the follow-up study, he awoke with lumps on various parts of the body. This was diagnosed in the emergency room as a rash due to hives. (Ms. Wilson's experience with hives was several months prior to this.)

Ms. Wilson reported to the pediatrician doing the follow-up examination that Johnny had had the recommended infant and child immunizations at the proper ages. When Johnny was seen, he appeared quiet, cheerful, and cooperative. Aside from slightly reduced hearing in one ear, he had no medical problems; but his nails were bitten short, he revealed impaired right-left discrimination, and he could not tell time.

Johnny scored unusually low on the Piers-Harris Children's Self Concept Scale. The clinician judged that the child would benefit from a great deal of support. Johnny's responses to the dramatic role-play stimuli and his use of puppets revealed unusual creativity and ability to plan and carry out stories. He was seen as a potentially able child with greater than average talent and skill.

According to Johnny's school records, psychological tests administered in kindergarten had shown him of average intellectual ability and ready to enter first grade, although he was younger than the average beginning first grader. His first-grade performance, however, was barely passing, and he continued to learn at a minimal level in the next two grades.

Late in the spring of Johnny's third grade, he came to the attention of a pediatrician in a local hospital, who became concerned at his poor grades and involved the school social worker to help. Ms. Wilson also showed interest and began going over Johnny's lessons with him. Johnny not only improved but produced an A paper in science, much to the astonishment of school personnel. Clearly, he had greater ability than he had revealed to date.

At the end of our follow-up study, the staff felt that Johnny needed much encouragement and support along with goals that he might realistically achieve. The school social worker was happy to re-enter the situation, and it looked as though Johnny might get the sustained individual attention he had missed. Unfortunately, Ms. Wilson saw no need for continued work with any school personnel. She reported that Johnny was now bringing home A and B papers and seemed at last to be profiting from school attendance. It was not until several months later that we received a late communication from the school and learned that his grades were actually at the lowest level ever. By this time the interviewers had left the study and it was not possible to visit Ms. Wilson at home. It is doubtful anyway that a few more visits would have changed the situation.

At no time during our limited contacts with the Wilson family did we feel that Johnny was abused. The stroller accident that brought the family to our attention was understandable in a situation where a mother must care for three preschoolers. Some grounds did exist for considering Johnny neglected: Ms. Wilson's failure to obtain standard immunizations, Johnny's inadvertent ingestion of poison (if true), and the absence of a structure and reasonable guidelines for his socialization. On the other side of the ledger was Ms. Wilson's fondness of her son, seen in her steady visits to him in the hospital, her provision of whatever material goods she could afford, and her pleasure in describing him. One might speculate that the tie between Johnny and his mother was, if anything, too strong. Thus Ms. Wilson's lack of motivation and goals was being instilled in Johnny and was leading to a waste of his potential. When we saw him, Johnny was still responsive to individual attention, but he could not sustain his output when the attention stopped. In the present family situation his future is anything but promising.

Much about Ms. Wilson elicits sympathy. Her reliance on Children's Hospital for someone to talk to implies a frightening lack of environmental support. In similar fashion, her need to see everything in the most positive terms bespeaks a woman whose life is barren of normal satisfactions. Apparently she cannot tolerate deficiencies in herself: she must report that all of Johnny's immunizations were completed properly and that she has known of her high blood pressure only a few months. Her fantasized description of Johnny's father fits the same pattern. Ms. Wilson shows a limited capacity to deal with reality. Although this causes many problems for her, it is crippling for Johnny, because she persists in thinking he is doing well when he is scraping bottom.

The difficulties in helping families like the Wilsons are manifest. Probably the best entrance would be through Johnny, whose real gifts might be nurtured by a sensitive leader in a recreation or activity group. Without some form of environmental stimulation, Johnny is likely to develop into a male Ms. Wilson, passive, restricted, and emotionally impoverished.

Jill Barry: A Comparison Case

Jill, a white girl aged eight and a half, was chosen as a comparison child on the basis of her hospitalization with a viral infection at the age of six months. Child Welfare Services confirmed that she had never been reported abused. Mrs. Barry willingly made an appointment to see the interviewer.

Mrs. Barry was a thirty-year-old housewife, the mother of five children of whom the oldest was eleven. Jill was the second child and the first girl; the younger children were two girls and a boy. All had difficulties of one kind and another. The older boy had what Mrs. Barry described as a "lazy eye," and Jill had had an operation at the age of three because her eyes turned in. The third child was so hyperactive that she was considered a problem both at home and at school. The fourth child suffered from bronchial asthma, and the youngest, aged three, had occasional febrile seizures.

Mrs. Barry appeared tense, nervous, and somewhat anxious not only during the initial interview but also on each subsequent contact. The interviewer felt that she never fully understood the whole family situation as Mrs. Barry appeared to have something on her mind that she could not talk about. She was a high-school graduate who had never been employed and who seemed overwhelmed by the task of bringing up five children, all born within the space of eight years. Mrs. Barry's activities were confined to keeping the house, managing the children, and putting meals on the table. She had very few outside activities and mentioned only one social group in which she was interested. Although both sets of grandparents lived within walking distance, there was no indication of a warm relationship between any of them and the Barrys.

Mr. Barry also was a high-school graduate. He made his living as a truck driver, which necessitated being out of town much of the time. He had a comfortable and predictable income but did little to help with the day-by-day management of the household. When he did come home from his long trips, he enjoyed watching television or playing with the children. Mrs. Barry described him as able to calm down the children, a capacity that she envied.

Despite a relatively adequate income, the family lived in a run-down neighborhood that included several condemned dwellings. The interior of the house was reasonably neat and clean but lacked touches that convey a personal sense of the household members.

The most striking aspect of the family portrait was Mrs. Barry's medical history. Early in her twenties she had been hospitalized for three weeks for the removal of gallstones. Jill was born about a year later. Shortly thereafter, Mrs. Barry contracted a bladder infection that persisted several years despite extensive medical treatment and a number of hospitalizations. It was not cleared up until the birth of the last child. A couple of years before we became acquainted with the family, Mrs. Barry had had a complete hysterectomy. A year later she developed ulcers for which she was still taking tranquilizers. Aside from hospitalizations for deliveries, Mrs. Barry had been a hospital inpatient approximately twenty times. Fortunately for her and the family, one of the grandmothers had been available to care for the children on each of these many occasions.

Mrs. Barry described herself as a high-strung person who became overwrought at times because of her responsibilities. When angry, she was inclined to hit out at people and frequently had attacked Mr. Barry physically. He never retaliated, a fact that Mrs. Barry found remarkable. As she went on to describe the discipline of the children, the interviewer gained the impression that she was very free in the use of a paddle. This was the treatment she chose for almost any transgression by any one of the children.

Mrs. Barry was preoccupied with Jill's difficulties. She said that Jill still sucked her thumb even though she was almost nine years old. She cried easily, sometimes several times a day; Mrs. Barry found it hard to tolerate this behavior. Jill often appeared sad and complained that she was picked on by her parents, particularly her mother. She seemed more sensitive than the other children and needed considerable praise to keep her going. Recently she had begun to lie about little things and appeared unable to stop. She was openly rivalrous with her older brother and next younger sister and attempted to dominate them in various subtle and overt ways. For example, she refused to take her younger sister to the neighborhood recreation center unless the little girl made Jill's bed.

Jill had always been the slowest of the children. She had refused to give up the bottle, the crib, her favorite blanket, and was not toilet trained until way beyond the age that Mrs. Barry thought appropriate. However, she seemed to enjoy games appropriate for her age such as jump rope, hopscotch, riding a bicycle, playing house, and swimming at the neighborhood center.

School had always been a problem for Jill. She hated to go and frequently begged off by pleading illness. Other times she would go to school but would return early because of nausea. On these occasions she seemed to develop good health by afternoon. The mother had observed that Jill could make herself vomit. Mrs. Barry thought the child was fearful of tests and unduly anxious about failing.

At the time of this interview the school problems appeared to be diminishing because Jill had moved into a new classroom where she was a little more comfortable. According to school records she had always done acceptable work. At the same time her desperate competition with her siblings had increased to the extent that at one time she hid in her bedroom when her younger sister received a present and she did not. She refused to come out for several hours and lay on her bed pathetically sobbing.

In talking about the development of a moral sense, Mrs. Barry thought that most children knew right from wrong at approximately three to four years. Jill had been slower than this but did now seem to be aware of what was right. Whenever she broke any of the house rules, Mrs. Barry spanked her. Mr. Barry was even more inclined to use the stick than Mrs. Barry. The mother saw Jill as immature and not very responsible and, consequently, never left her alone, even to go to the neighborhood store a block away.

When the pediatrician saw Mrs. Barry to obtain Jill's medical history as part of the follow-up study, a bit more of the early history was filled in. Jill had been born three weeks early and from the beginning had exhibited feeding problems shown in frequent vomiting and refusal to eat. She did not improve until she was almost two years old. The pediatrician noted all the problems that had already been mentioned by Mrs. Barry, namely, a tendency on the part of Jill to somatize, much difficulty in getting along with her siblings, and separation problems related to her mother. Another observation was that Mrs. Barry seemed to be "sitting on her anger."

A winsome child with long blond hair, Jill at this point was well developed and well nourished, although she had poor alternating hand motions and intermittent esophoria (tendency of the eyes to

turn in). When Jill was asked about the reason for her eye operation several years before, she replied that her sister had injured
her. (Since there was no evidence of such an injury, we assumed
Jill's statement to be a projection of her own hostility against her
sister.)

Jill made us a drawing of a little girl with long hair. The body,
hands, and feet showed excellent detail. The child was Jill's age;
she felt lonely because she had no friends. When asked what the
little girl in the picture was doing, Jill announced she would give
the child something to do, and she drew a jump rope in the hands
of the child. She next drew a companion, an almost identical figure
standing next to the first one and also holding a jump rope.

In the dramatic role play, Jill's first three stories were brief and
imaginative. Beginning with the stimulus about the crocodile and
the crow (Appendix 3a), Jill started to make the characters drown,
be chewed up, get sick and die, be hung in the cellar, or engage in
sexual activities only thinly disguised. As the stories went on, she
grew increasingly verbal, excited, and fanciful. Her sixth story, the
entirely spontaneous one, was three times the length of either the
first or the second one. It involved four actors in a complicated tale
that shifted from one location to another. By this time Jill had
become thoroughly involved in the activity and went on to spin out
still another spontaneous production. The cast included a mother
and a father, two boys, two girls, and a baby. People played hug-
ging games either standing up or lying down. Some of the fantasied
individuals understood the game but others were mystified, became angry, and ran away or hid. Actors from the earlier stories
were recalled and woven into the new tale, which ended with the
father and the mother stuffed into the king and everybody "having
fun." The clinician interpreted these stories as manifestations of
Jill's intense feelings of anger, sexuality, and competition in relation to other family members. Jill was seen as a bright, imaginative,
and complex child who needed help to deal with her conflicting
emotions.

According to our language specialist, Jill's language development was good. However, she had a rasping voice (tallied as a communication problem), and her spontaneous stories, like those above, were filled with violence.

When the staff reviewed the findings for Jill, it was apparent that she could well use outside help. The examiners agreed that she had many strengths but her energies were being devoured by her psychological difficulties. We decided to discuss with Mrs. Barry the possibility of a referral to a local mental health clinic for both herself and Jill.

Mrs. Barry eagerly accepted this referral. She went on to say that she had hoped Jill's problems would be diagnosed and that something could be done for her as a result of participation in the follow-up study. She had even considered getting psychiatric help for the child but did not know if the difficulties were serious enough for what she regarded as a major step. She had also hoped that Jill would outgrow the various problems, but instead they seemed to be getting worse. Within a week the clinic was in touch with us requesting information because Mrs. Barry and Jill had applied for service.

We have less information about the comparison families including the Barrys, than the families of the traumatized children because the comparison families had not been seen prior to the follow-up study. Also, Mrs. Barry did appear to have something on her mind that she was reluctant to divulge to the interviewer, who was in no position to establish a strong relationship with her. Nevertheless we might speculate that the birth of five children within eight years, followed by numerous severe health problems, had contributed much to Mrs. Barry's difficulties with her children. Jill's birth was both preceded and followed by a major illness of the mother. Jill's early and persistent feeding difficulties as well as her need to remain an infant might well have resulted from Mrs. Barry's preoccupation with her own physical condition.

The nature and extent of Mrs. Barry's illnesses suggest a psychological as well as an organic component. Support for this idea is found in Jill's attempts to escape school through somatization, a mechanism that her mother may have modeled for her. Each of the five children had some kind of dysfunction, either physical or neurological, a fact that probably added to Mrs. Barry's woes.

We saw no evidence of abuse or neglect in the family; and neither did we perceive an undue amount of violent behavior, with the exception of Mrs. Barry's attacks on her husband and possibly the overly free use of the paddle on the children. The only environmental stress appeared to be the deteriorated neighborhood and even this was not a subject of complaint. Despite the apparent absence of empathetic relationships with the grandparents, in a pinch they took on the responsibility of the children, thus providing a needed cushion of support.

The limited amount of data concerning Jill and her young age make it difficult to assess how embedded her psychological troubles might be. Hopeful signs are her ability to relate to the examiners in the follow-up study, her adequate school achievement, and Mrs. Barry's recognition of the need for help and ability to utilize available resources.

CHAPTER 4

Conclusion

Like marital infidelity and prostitution, child abuse is a social phenomenon of some magnitude, but while the former are winked at by society, abuse is unambiguously condemned. Private citizens and professionals alike are bent on establishing the true nature of the problem, protecting the children, and rehabilitating the families. This chapter directs attention to the implications of this study in relation to these broad goals.

To attack a problem, one must first ascertain its nature, then choose appropriate weapons. We see abuse as one point on a continuum of child care practices ranging from exceptionally good through adequate to exceptionally poor. In between are practices that may have results ranging from physical illness or behavioral problems in the child to accidents, neglect, or abuse.

The child care practices of most families across the entire social spectrum fluctuate around adequate — at times very good, at other times just good enough, and occasionally poor enough to result in reactive illness of the child or minor accidents. Many variables influence child care, for example, the amount of social stress perceived by the parents and the balance between stress and support. As we know, abusive parents perceive (and also may be truly subject to) greater stress than nonabusive families. At the same time abusive families have a sketchier support system and are, thus, rendered more vulnerable to stress. Abusive families, of course, do not abuse continuously; rather, because of the stress-support imbalance, their child care practices may fluctuate over a wider continuum than is true of nonabusive families.

However, despite the clear differences as to stress and support between the abusive and the accident families at Time One, we found few differences among the children. As mentioned in chapter 2, the similarity of findings for all the groups forced us to the judgment that some common factor must be contributing to the children's widespread difficulties, and we identified this as most of the families' membership in the lower social classes, or, for those who had moved up, the strains of lower-class membership during the children's early years and a continuing lack of stable and supportive family life.

The effects of poverty (or lower-class membership) on children are devastating. Birch and Gussow (1970) state that poor children are not only born *into* poverty, they are also born *of* it. That is, the pregnant mother may not get enough to eat and often seeks little or no medical care. From infancy on, poverty affects physical development, health, the development of language, intellectual achievement, and behavior. The findings of many investigators document these conclusions. For example, analyses of data from schools throughout the United States show that children from the lower classes, of whatever race, performed poorly on most measures of academic achievement (Coleman et al., 1966). Further, as disadvantaged children progress through the educational system, academic failure becomes more pronounced. This may lead to limited education because of early dropping out, which in turn results in limited employment opportunities. Thus, poverty reinforces and perpetuates itself from one generation to another (Birch and Gussow, 1970).

Werner et al. (1971) studied a group of children born in Kauai, one of the Hawaiian Islands, and found that the quality of the environment was the major determinant of physical, intellectual, and emotional status by the time the child was ten. Similar findings have been reported by Duncan, Young, and Kirkwood (1974), who found that the school a child attended was less important for adequate achievement than the home he came from. Davie (1973) followed seventeen thousand children born in 1958 in England and reported a marked and consistent relationship between the occupational status (social class) of their fathers and most aspects of the children's behavior, development, and ability.

By placing the results of our follow-up study in the context of the massive literature concerning poverty, we come to the conclusion that the results of child abuse are less potent for the child's development than class membership. In turn, this suggests that one crucial method to protect children is a full-scale, coordinated attack upon poverty. Part of any such program should consist of children's services designed for the entire population of minors, not simply lower-class children. Schorr (1974) has amassed impressive evidence that current children's programs, because they serve chiefly the disadvantaged groups, are inadequate, uncoordinated, fragmented, and underfunded. And Rodham (1973) has noted a cultural recalcitrance in the United States toward assuming public responsibility for children's needs. To quote Jenkins, "children's needs are universal but they are met in a selective way" (1974, p. 3). Curiously, one of the major aims of current programs addressed to abuse is to coordinate and maximize the variety of services available to abusive families. One has to inquire why parents must abuse a child to be eligible for well-thought-out services.

The association of most children's services with the lower classes means that families may use them reluctantly because of the attached stigma. But, in addition, commonly available services tend not to address the realistic needs of young families — for example, support for the mother of the first-born when she leaves the hospital; information concerning what to expect from an infant; special support in times of stress in the form of drop-off nurseries or home aides; and parent-child centers where parents can help one another if need be or simply relax and chat. Making such services available without the equivalent of a means test would do much toward helping parents, even without attacking ills caused by poverty. When support is increased, the perception of stress is often reduced to manageable proportions.

What should be the role of the law in the protection of children from mistreatment? A brief review shows that state laws are constantly being expanded regarding both who is to report and what is to be reported. Many states have central registries in which reports of abuse are mechanically stored for the benefit of a few sources or an array of professional individuals or agencies. The primary purpose of storing such reports is to ensure help for the family; the assumption is that care and treatment do follow the report. Sussman and Cohen (1975) made a detailed study of the issues involved in reporting child maltreatment. Their initial premise was that child abuse and, to a lesser extent, child neglect could be ameliorated by requiring reports of suspected abuse defined in relatively broad terms. The investigators revised this hypothesis because they observed that undue emphasis on reporting seemed to serve to divert attention from more pervasive social problems, of which child mistreatment could be a symptom. They also found that treatment did not automatically follow reporting. Remedial services were often substandard and underfunded. Even adequate treatment programs frequently could not provide services conducive to the physical and psychological well-being of the abused or neglected child and his or her family. This was especially true when the services included coercive removal of a child from his own home. The authors concluded that, in such cases, a child's liberty and the loss of custody by the parents were being traded for a promise of treatment seldom achieved. They ended by recommending mandatory reporting only in cases of serious physical injury.

The present writer concurs with the conclusions of Sussman and Cohen for reasons that will be discussed shortly. But there is another possible role for the law in relation to abuse, and that is expansion and standardization of the statutes for the termination of parental rights. Despite the best efforts of qualified and knowledgeable clinicians, some parents cannot achieve even a minimally acceptable level of child care. The unhappy fact is that we do not know enough to help certain very damaged parents. For the sake of their children, we need legal termination mechanisms that protect the rights of parents as fairly as possible while at the same time ensuring a good environment for young children, whose developmental needs cannot wait.

One step in this direction is the Parental Stress Center of Pittsburgh, of which this writer is director of research and training. One of the Center's aims is to assist in the development of equitable termination statutes. The court mandates abused or high-risk infants of one year or less to the Center for residential care. Parents visit daily to care for their babies under staff supervision. Our primary goal is to augment the child-rearing abilities of parents so they may be reunited with their offspring. We make extensive observations and collect detailed information concerning the parent-child interaction and the parents' response to the program as a whole. These data form the basis of our recommendations to the court for placement of the babies following their stay with us, which usually lasts about three months. Ultimately, we hope to be able to define the characteristics of parents who can be rehabilitated with the aid of our program and the characteristics of parents who are beyond our power to help. Such profiles should contribute to more realistic standards for termination when this proves necessary.

But the Parental Stress Center, like many other current programs, addresses abuse after the fact, when even picking up the pieces is difficult. Remediation must be attempted, of course, and we cannot afford to abandon the effort. Nonetheless, as knowledge about abuse and about child-rearing practices in general has accumulated, the conviction has grown that remediation is not enough: the focus on child abuse is too narrow and does not begin to help parents in the early stages of distress that may lead to abuse.

The volume of reported cases of child abuse in this country is rising astronomically and is projected to reach one million incidents a year very shortly. Such numbers simply cannot be dealt with through the present reporting-investigating-legal system, which is already grievously overburdened. In some large cities a plan of triage has been adopted, meaning that only the most serious cases of abuse are investigated. If a family is reported and then finds that little or nothing is done by the authorities, the parents could easily draw the inference that nobody really cares how they manage their children. In turn, this inference would reinforce their deviant child care methods. This is an unforeseen side effect of the present system.

The hundreds of thousands of reports of suspected abuse now pouring in from everywhere indicate that the mistreatment of children is so widespread that it should be considered a substantial aspect of Western culture, a cultural deviation quite distinct from individual pathology. Other evidence is the common utilization of physical punishment for children, even infants. Korsch, Christian, Gozzi, and Carlson (1965) have found that a large proportion of clinic mothers use corporal punishment to teach babies under the age of one, and our own studies, reported in Wittenberg (1971), have demonstrated that mothers of every social class employ such punishment for infants. The practice does not result in guilty feelings; parents openly state that physical punishment will "show the child who's boss."

The history of the punishment or mistreatment of children has been well detailed by Radbill (1968). Suffice it to say that from antiquity until approximately one hundred years ago, there was overwhelming support for the concept that children are the property of their parents and must be made to submit to their will. Children in ancient civilizations, even when grown, could be put to death, sold into slavery, or bartered on the open market by their fathers. In industrial England they could be indentured as early as the age of three and goaded into work by beatings. Early in the history of our own country, eminent theologians termed children "young vipers" and preached the doctrine of childhood depravity, which could be erased only by thrashing the child to break his will. Thus, history, advice, and experience have contributed to great pressure to utilize physical punishment to bring children into line. Small wonder that so many parents today are convinced of its utility and rightness.

Another aspect of the problem is the high expectations, often quite unrealistic, that parents commonly hold with regard to their children. A study of men in prison for physical violence toward a child revealed they punished the child out of exasperation at his or her failure to progress (Gibbens and Walker, 1956). Ignorance of normal psychological development is especially striking when the child in question is an infant. The parents may believe the baby is a thinking, scheming individual who could stop crying if he so desired, eat neatly, become toilet trained, and sleep all night. When the child does not behave acceptably, it is easy for parents espousing such beliefs to blame him for being obstinate and willful. Here again, history, advice, and experience have had a part in etching high expectations into the minds of caretakers. For many centuries children were perceived as little adults. They were portrayed in sculpture and painting as small men and women with well-formed features and erect postures. Especially among highborn families, children's clothes were more appropriate for their elders, and they were encouraged to indulge in adult activities. The idea of childhood as a developmental stage was unknown until the past five or six decades.

Clearly, any infant is bound to thwart the unrealistically high expectations of his parents merely by virtue of being a baby. When the disappointed parent subscribes to socialization by physical punishment, the potential for trouble is high. At worst the result may be injury or death; at best, the beginning of a relationship of force, parent against child. It should be emphasized that high expectations and the use of physical punishment are not peculiar to abusive parents, but are embedded in the child care methods of a very large population of well-meaning caretakers.

The two cultural phenomena, unrealistic expectations and physical punishment for babies, offer a starting point for a nonlegal method to reduce mistreatment and also to drain off some of the potential for abuse. One technique is a saturation educational campaign via the mass media. Most parents want to do their best with their infants and young children. They are more open to advice at this stage than any other period of their child-rearing years since parent-child relationships have not yet become firmly established. A media campaign offers an opportunity to bring into consciousness some of the illogical and inappropriate expectations adults have of babies. At present, parents have few sources of information on such matters because they assume — as does society — that they already know. On the other hand, pediatricians, nurses, social workers, and others who come into contact with young mothers mistakenly assume that all young children are kindly nurtured. The fact is, infants frequently learn the hard way through being spanked, swatted, shaken, and beaten, to say nothing of being deprived and isolated for misdeeds of which they are totally unaware.

While much is expected of mothers, there is little attempt to provide needed information or resources, such as day care or home help. Motherhood as it now exists in this country seems to have institutionalized the worst aspects of the role: isolation and lack of help, support, and knowledge. Many mothers and much of society feel mothers rightfully bear total responsibility for the product (Bernard, 1974). It seems that while everyone is willing to point a finger, no one is willing to extend a hand.

Advocacy for children's rights is currently causing an exciting ferment in the courts and our social institutions, but the achievement of legal rights will be hollow unless adults can be persuaded to change their historical beliefs and practices in relation to children and become more aware of the realities of parenthood, especially motherhood. Mass-media education appears to hold promise, provided it can be mounted attractively and with a light touch. Other efforts are also promising, for example, Kempe's proposal (1976) for health visitors to assist new parents from the birth of a child through the preschool years; Schneider, Hoffmeister, and Helfer's predictive questionnaire (1976) to identify at-risk parents and their newborns; and education for parenthood (now being offered in some schools and communities). The involvement of physicians, especially pediatricians, in preventive efforts is much to be desired. Their standing in the community plus their intimate contacts with young parents place them in a position to exert powerful influence for change.

The mistreatment of children, including abuse and neglect, has multiple determinants, and no one preventive effort will be able to solve the problem completely. Perhaps most important of all are our own attitudes, as expressed so well by Hobbs:

> *In the thinness of community, restoration of a common commitment to children becomes increasingly urgent. If I neglect my child, your child will pay for my neglect ten times over. If a child goes to bed hungry, we are all diminished by his distress. When a rat bites a child at night, it bites all sleeping children. And you and I are responsible. (Hobbs, 1976, italics added)*

Appendices
Notes
Bibliography
Index

Appendix 1a

Stability Index and Scoring System, T_1-T_2

Item		Score
1. Mother living with husband or boyfriend	0	No
	2	Yes
2. Adequate income[a]	0	No
	2	Yes
3. Private source of income	0	No
	1	Yes
4. Family moves since conception of index child	0	> 2 moves
	1	2 moves
	2	< 2 moves
5. Mother's health	0	High risk
	1	Moderate risk
	2	No risk
6. Family stress	0	High stress
	1	Moderate stress
	2	Low stress
	3	No reported stress
7. Continuity of care of index child	0	No
	2	Yes

[a] Standards used were those of the U.S. Bureau of the Census for 1966. To be considered adequate, income had to be greater than poverty level for the number in the family.

Appendix 1b

Support Index and Scoring System, T_1-T_2

Item		*Score*
1. Availability of a person to confide in	0	No
	2	Yes
2. Male partner available	0	No
	1	Occasionally
	2	Yes
3. Expressed dissatisfaction with male partner	0	Dissatisfied
	1	Mixed
	2	Content
4. Availability of help from friends or neighbors	0	No
	1	Yes
5. Importance of religion	0	None
	1	Moderate
	2	Vital
6. Uses regular source of medical care for child	0	No source
	1	Intermittent
	2	Regular

Appendix 2a

Introductory Letter
to Infant Accident Study Families, T$_3$

Several years ago you were kind enough to take part in the Infant Accident Study. As you may remember, this was a study of the development of young children who were seen at Children's Hospital from 1965 through 1967.

We have always hoped to see the families and children again. We are now able to do this, and we are happy to offer a modest sum for your help.

Within the next two or three weeks two members of our staff, Mrs. Orris and Mr. Miller, will be in touch with you to enlist your cooperation if possible. We hope that you and your child will again wish to participate. The study is sponsored by the Pittsburgh Child Guidance Center and Children's Hospital.

Sincerely,

Appendix 2b

Stability Index and Scoring System, T_3

Item		Score
1. Mother living with husband or boyfriend	0	No
	2	Yes
2. Adequate income[a]	0	No
	2	Yes
3. Private source of income	0	No
	1	Yes
4. Family moves in past five years	0	> 2 moves
	1	2 moves
	2	< 2 moves
5. Mother's health	0	High risk
	1	Moderate risk
	2	No risk
6. Family stress	0	High stress
	1	Moderate stress
	2	Low stress
	3	No reported stress
7. Continuity of care of index child	0	No
	2	Yes

[a] Standards used were those of the U.S. Bureau of the Census for 1974. To be considered adequate, income had to be greater than poverty level for the number in the family.

Appendix 2c

Source of Support, T_3

Case # _____
Scored by _____
Date _____

Types of Support	Immediate Family				Extended Family			Others	Religion	Professionals	Other Groups (1)	TOTAL
	Husband or Boyfriend (2)	Parents/In-Laws (1)	Children ≥ 18 (1)	Children < 18 (.5)	Grandparents (1)	Siblings (1)	Other Relatives (1)	Friends or Baby-Sitter (1)	Clergy, Religious Groups, or Lord (1)	Other Individuals or Agencies (1)		
Household management (1)												
Confide, talk (2)												
Care of children (1)												
Transportation (1)												
Family problems (1)												
Unspecified support (.5)												
TOTAL												

Husband or boyfriend present: YES _____ NO _____

Appendix 2d

Child Offenses and Maternal Reactions

Case # _____
Rated by _____
Date _____

Offense	Physical punishment	Threatens physical punishment	Isolation	Deprivation of privileges	Other inappropriate actions	Negative verbal	Reason, advise, warn	Other appropriate actions	No response from mother, ignoring	Punishment—type not specified	TOTAL
Missing school Yes No UK											
Poor school performance Yes No UK											
Forgetfulness Yes No UK											
Destroying property Yes No UK											
Lying Yes No UK											
Hitting mother Yes No UK											
Other offenses Yes No UK											
Acting upset Yes No UK											
Safety violations Yes No UK											
TOTAL											

Appendix 2e

Your Child–Most Children Questionnaire, T₃

Please check the blank you think best describes your child:

1. How often does your child obey you?

Most of the time	A good bit of the time	A moderate amount	Not often	Not at all

2. When your child can't do something, how often would he/she keep on trying?

Most of the time	A good bit of the time	A moderate amount	Not often	Not at all

3. How much of the time is he/she angry?

Most of the time	A good bit of the time	A moderate amount	Not often	Not at all

4. How willing is your child to try new things?

A great deal	A good bit	A moderate amount	Very little	None

5. How often does your child try to do the right thing?

Most of the time	A good bit of the time	A moderate amount	Not often	Not at all

6. How often will your child work for something he/she wants?

Most of the time	A good bit of the time	A moderate amount	Not often	Not at all

7. How often does your child understand what you have to say to him?

Most of the time	A good bit of the time	A moderate amount	Not often	Not at all

8. How often does your child speak well enough so you can understand him?

Most of the time	A good bit of the time	A moderate amount	Not often	Not at all

9. How often is your child able to explain his ideas completely?

Most of the time	A good bit of the time	A moderate amount	Not often	Not at all

10. How often is your child able to talk about his feelings?

Most of the time	A good bit of the time	A moderate amount	Not often	Not at all

You probably have some ideas of what other children are like at this age. Please check the blank you think best describes most children.

1. How often do you think most children obey the mother?

Most of the time	A good bit of the time	A moderate amount	Not often	Not at all

2. When most children can't do something, how often do you think they would keep on trying?

Most of the time	A good bit of the time	A moderate amount	Not often	Not at all

3. How much of the time do you think most children are angry?

Most of the time	A good bit of the time	A moderate amount	Not often	Not at all

4. How willing are most children to try new things?

A great deal	A good bit	A moderate amount	Very little	None

5. How often do you think most children try to do the right thing?

Most of the time	A good bit of the time	A moderate amount	Not often	Not at all

6. How often do you think most children will work for something they want?

Most of the time	A good bit of the time	A moderate amount	Not often	Not at all

7. How often do most children understand what you have to say to them?

Most of the time	A good bit of the time	A moderate amount	Not often	Not at all

8. How often do most children speak well enough so you can understand them?

Most of the time	A good bit of the time	A moderate amount	Not often	Not at all

9. How often are most children able to explain their ideas completely?

Most of the time	A good bit of the time	A moderate amount	Not often	Not at all

10. How often are most children able to talk about their feelings?

Most of the time	A good bit of the time	A moderate amount	Not often	Not at all

Appendix 3a

Role-Play Stimulus Paragraphs

Story 1. Two boys are playing ball. One boy hits the ball very hard and it goes out of the field into this man's tomato patch. The boy goes after it and just as he's about to pick up the ball, he feels a swat on his backside. He looks up and sees the man standing there. What do you think happens?

Story 2. Two boys [girls] are playing ball in the living room. One boy throws the ball hard and it hits a lamp. The lamp falls and breaks. Just then they hear the mother coming from the kitchen into the living room. What do you think happens?

Story 3. Two boys [girls] are in school and one of the boys is a teaser. He's always teasing the other boy. One day they're taking a test and the boy sees the teaser looking at his paper. He covers his paper, and just then he sees the teaser sticking out his tongue and making a terrible face at him. What do you think happens?

Story 4. Suppose that this crow has lived all his life by the pond, and every day he goes to the pond to drink the fresh water and eat the berries along the bank. One day he goes for his usual dinner and he sees this crocodile eating the berries and drinking the water. What happens?

Story 5. Suppose that this is a witch who lives in the forest. Every night she goes to town and takes all the townspeople's stuff. One day this man goes into the forest to gather firewood with his pet. He goes very far and it gets late; he realizes that he won't get back to the village and will have to sleep in the forest. He also knows the witch lives in the forest. What happens?

Story 6. This story was a spontaneous invention by the child.

Appendix 3b

Stories Told by an Eight-Year-Old White Accident Girl

Role-Play Stimulus Story 2

Examiner: [Gives stimulus paragraph.] Did he break any lamps or windows this time?

Child: Yeah. And he said, "We won't break nothing." The other boys says, "Right." So when they were catching the ball, the ball hit over to along where it broke — it was a hard ball. And the father comes running down the stairs saying, "What was that big crash?" And they said, "Nothing!" And when he says, "Well, I want to go mow the lawn" [actually "lawn the mow"] and when he was getting ready to push it, the whole thing fell apart and they said, "Was that the crash that I heard?" The boys say, "Yeah." "Well, you dirty boys you get up in your beds and tomorrow you're not going to play ball and don't come down till suppertime." So they went in their bed and they ate supper and then the next day they were playing football outside. They were playing football and the football ran over to this lady that was hanging out her clothes and her whole line of clothes fell down and hit her on her head and she looked and she make sure she saw those boys cause the last time she told them to play football and the lady said, "Did your football come in my yard?" and they said, "Yeah," and they said, "I'm sorry," and the lady said, "Wait till I tell your mother and father." So she went over and told their mother and their father, and they had to go up to bed again. And this time they weren't allowed to do nothing but stay in bed all day or stay in the house. So the next day they stayed in the house and they were jumping on their beds. They had bunk beds and they were jumping. The boy on top caved in, fell into the other bed on the bottom and he went right through the floor, right through all the floors, down to the cellar. When their mother saw that big mess, she could have killed them. So then one day they decided to kill their boys and get a few girls and they did and she grew up now.

E.: Did the father help the mother kill the two boys and get the girls?

C.: Yeah.

E.: Are the girls neater and cleaner than the boys?

C.: They help their mother in the kitchen and they drop everything.

E.: And what does the mother think about that?

C.: She gets rid of them and that's all.

E.: Did she get any more children?

C.: No, but one time when the father got through with the lawn-mower he broke it and he decided to kill himself, and the mother dropped the food on the kitchen floor and she decided to kill herself. And there was nobody.

Role-Play Stimulus Story 3

Examiner: [Gives stimulus paragraph.]

Child: When she was turning her pencil, her head, around she missed two questions and she didn't even know. And then they got another one, and when the other girl . . . when her teacher was checking her test and she saw she missed two she said, "Why did you miss both of these?" And she said, "The teaser was teasing me so I turned around and I missed two," so they went home. They asked their mom if they could help her. Mom said, "Yeah" and their mother said, "Why don't you help with the supper?" and the girl said, "OK, I like to cook," so both of them cooked, and when they were cooking the girl was cutting the potatoes and the teaser came up and pushed her and was teasing her and she dropped the potatoes on the floor and they got all dirty and her mother came in and saw those potatoes on the floor and she said, "What! How did those potatoes get on the floor?" She said, "The teaser pushed me and was teasing me" and she said to the teaser, "Go up to your room." So she went up to her room and so the other girl was cooking and they were having chicken. It all came out of the pan and dropped on the floor and onto her stockings she was wearing stockings. There was two big holes in her stockings and her mother came in and said, "Where did you get those holes in, where is that chicken in the oven?" She didn't tell her the chicken was in the oven so she cleaned it up and threw it away. And the pan was cooking and when the mother took it out it was all ashes and she said, "What happened to all that chicken that I had in here? Do you suppose it burnt?" And the little girl said, "Maybe" and the mother said, "Well, cook it again — chicken don't become ashes." She looked and said, "Did the chicken fall?" She said, "Yep," and we start all over again. And she had to go up to her bed, and her mother, when she was making the corn, she was cutting it and she was drinking some milk and she dropped the glass and broke the floor down and the glass broke and she said, "Well, I better go to bed too."

When the father came home, he had nothing to eat but dirty corn, ashes, and raw potatoes so he went upstairs and found them all sleeping and they woke up so they decided to go out to dinner. The little girls had spaghetti and they were slopping it all over. There was spaghetti all over their hair and everything and they were sticking the noodles around their wrist and around their legs for stockings and bracelets, and their mother and father were eating chicken — I mean beef stew. They were throwing the gravy all over each other because one had chicken stew and one had beef stew and the father wanted the chicken stew and the mother wanted it so he got the beef stew and they were throwing carrots and stuff all over and they were all dirty. So when they got home, they took a bath and they went to bed. The little girls didn't want to go to bed so they went downstairs and they were playing ball; the TV was on. When they were throwing the ball, the TV burned out and caved in the whole floor and they catched on fire, and they went upstairs in their bed because they snuck down, and when their mother and father came down, she saw that mess and they said, "We've got to get rid of those girls just like those dirty old boys. They can't keep nothing nice around the house." So the mother and father are living all alone and their father worked at a steel company, and one day he went in to make a new TV and he put one little tip of the steel on the porch. The whole house caved in so the mother got a new house and she was living all by herself and she got a dog and her dog always was biting her legs and everything and the dog ate her all up. And the dog was all alone and he teared all the stuff apart and he was so full he exploded and he was dead too.

E.: What do you think of that story, Sue?
C.: Funny
E.: Do you know anybody who makes big messes like that?
C.: Yeah, I know somebody like that.

Appendix 3c

Stories Told by a Nine-Year-Old White Abused Boy

Role-Play Stimulus Story 2

Examiner: [Gives stimulus paragraph.]

Child: I don't know how to do.

E.: Well, just as you did the last one. Pretend to talk for each one of the boys and pretend that they're throwing the ball back and forth and just talk as you think it might go.

C.: "Hey, Bob, can you catch this?" It broke a lamp. Uh oh, here comes mother. "Boys, who broke that lamp?" "He did, he did." "Which one of you broke it?" "I did." "You'll have to stay in for two weeks. You for one week. You both have to stay in for two weeks for playing ball in the house."

E.: What did the boys think about the punishment and staying in for two weeks?

C.: They think they deserve it.

E.: So they think it's OK for mom to punish them in that way.

Role-Play Stimulus Story 3

Examiner: [Gives stimulus paragraph.]

Child: "Hey, you looking on my paper?" . . . I can't do it.

E.: You can have him make a face and stick out his tongue.

C.: He gets mad and does it back. And then he starts fighting. "Boys, stop fighting! You'll have to, you two will have to stay in for recess today."

E.: And is that the way that story ends?

C.: Uh huh.

E.: How does this boy feel, the one who is being teased? He has to stay in.

C.: He's gonna beat him up after school.

Appendix 3d

Stories Told by a Nine-Year-Old Black Comparison Girl

Role-Play Stimulus Story 2

Examiner: OK. That's the end of story 1. Story 2 is about two girls and the mother. Here's the mother in the kitchen. Here are two girls in the living room. And you know what? They're playing ball . . . in the house.

Child: Oh, every time you bring out one of them, their faces are different.

E.: Do they look a little different to you?

C.: This girl is real dark and this one isn't.

E.: Yes. They do look a little different.

C.: She looks purple.

E.: Well, these two girls are in the living room. [Begins stimulus paragraph.] Here, you're looking at the mother and that's right. Just at that time the mother [continues with same paragraph]. What do you think happens?

C.: She say, "Come here." Oops. She told her to come here. She asked her where we ought to put it. Into the living room. And she looks at her mother and her mother say, "Answer me." And so, then, she answered her mother. She say, "I just wanted to have some fun." And she had to get on punishment. If she ain't, this girl go home. I . . .

E.: They keep falling over, huh?

C.: So this girl went home and she got on punishment and got a whipping. So she got home and her mother's arguing with her. Her mother's mad at her. And she got up, she had to go sit in her bedroom and stay there for two weeks. So she goes, 'Wweeeeppp," and the mother thinks about, and "I put her on punishment for two weeks." And then she calls her down again and she comes downstairs. And the mother says, "I'm sorry for hollering at you. You should know better, not to play in the house with a ball." And her mother, and she said, "OK." And so the next day the little girl comes over and the mother is in the church. And so the mother, she says, "Did you get in trouble?" She said, "No." And she said,

"I did. Cause my mother say I had no business staying at anybody's house. And so my mother said I have to pay for the lamp." "That's easy," she say. And so then they had to save up enough money to buy a lamp. Then when they say they got a . . . cause they put the money back and they didn't buy the lamp. They got mad and they wanted to go see the circus. Their money was still in the bank. So they went down to the bank and got their money. They had a argument and then . . .

E.: Who had an argument?

C.: These two girls.

E.: The two girlfriends?

C.: And so after they had their argument, the girls, this girl say, "I'm sorry," and this girl say, "I'm not." And so the mother, the mother say, "Where are you going now?" And the mother, the little girl say, "Well, we was trying to save up enough of money for a, we were . . . together." So she say, and then they're start to fight again.

E.: One of the girls wanted to save money for the lamp and the other one didn't?

C.: Yes. This one wanted to save money for the lamp and this one didn't.

E.: Who's this the mother of?

C.: This one.

E.: I see. OK. And this is the, this is the what? The house where the lamp got broken?

C.: Yeh.

E.: Uh huh. OK.

C.: And so the mother was very mad and she told her to go home. And her little girl was very sorry and her little girl had the money saved. And she gave her some of her money for the lamp. And so the other little girl came over again and said, "I'm sorry," to the mother. And then the mother said, "I'm sorry too." And so this girl's mother came over and they, they, they decided to have a party. And they have a party. And . . .

E.: So they all made up?

C.: Yeh.

E.: And that's the end of that story. OK. Now we have a story of two boys.

Role-Play Stimulus Story 3

Child: Let's make a story about two boys, the girls, and like a whole family.

E.: We can. You can do that later on, if you want to, when you have a chance to make up any story you want. OK? If that's the idea you want to do. Right now, we have just a few more stories where I'm going to start in the beginning and you do the end. And this particular story is about two boys in school and . . .

C.: And this could be the teacher.

E.: OK. Do you know what a teaser is?

C.: It's somebody who teases everybody.

E.: Yes. That's what this boy is. [Gives part of stimulus story.]

C.: So he tries to cover up his paper. He turns around like this.

E.: And just then the teaser [continues with same stimulus paragraph]. What happens next?

C.: The teacher comes and she says, "Well, what are you trying to do?" He says, "Nothing." He looks at the ground and she say, "Look up." And he looks up. So the sun is, the two boys. He's still doing his paper, this one. . . . The teacher says, "You're always teasing; I should call your mother." So she calls his mother. His mother comes down. Then mother says, "Why have you been teasing everybody?" And he gets all E's on his report card, when he gets his report card, tomorrow. And so his teacher was really mad at him. And so his mother, oops, so this boy, he got all A's. And this boy, he never came back to his school again because he always teases everybody. So he has to go to a different school and everybody teases him. So it was a difficult. . . . And that's the end of the story.

E.: It was a difficult thing. So the teaser couldn't come back to that school anymore, and he had to go to a different school.

C.: Where everybody teased him.

E.: And then everybody teased him. Did everybody at the school, the other school, tease him?

C.: Yeh.

E.: My goodness. Well, that was a difficult situation, wasn't it? OK. Now, we're going to use two puppets for the next one. This one and this one.

Appendix 3e

Scale for Scoring Role-Play Stories

A. *Impulsivity.* The extent to which a person gives in to feelings, thoughts, and needs of the moment without thinking through a situation and assessing the best course of action.

Scale Point	Definition of Scale Point
1	Complete inhibition of action; no evidence of search behavior. Apparent overcontrol of feelings and action; little movement.
2	Minute evidence of activity indicating lessened control of feelings and behaviors; small amount of movement breaking through reserve.
3	Spontaneous action expressed in ways that are appropriate for the situation.
4	Some mistakes, forgetting, or misjudgments, which may indicate haste in acting upon feelings and ideas. May get caught up in tangential aspects of the task, or may give up easily and pursue another idea or feeling.
5	Considerable evidence of thoughtlessness, hasty actions, and misjudgments. May indicate loose ego boundaries and poor sense of self. Tangential thinking and distractible thought processes.

B. *Aggression.* Behavior that aims to inflict injury or pain on others; coercive use of power to manipulate or harm self or others; defense of self against undue pressure, harm, or coercion. May be expressed in verbal, nonverbal, or physical ways.

Scale Point	Definition of Scale Point
1	Avoidance of power, coercion, or manipulation; no evidence of verbal, nonverbal, or physical abuse.
2	Covert use of power. Indirect evidence of guilt feelings in relation to controlling others through self-injurious behavior. Some evidence of assertive behavior.
3	Evidence of appropriate self-assertiveness. Defends self or point of view, and/or punishes others in appropriate ways.
4	Power, coercion, or assertive behavior expressed in excess of what may be called for in the situation, e.g., yelling instead of explaining or hitting instead of smacking, resulting in psychic or physical harm to others.
5	Extreme use of power, coercion, or physical force. Global expression of injury: "overkill," catastrophes, annihilations. Grandiose fantasies of power and omnipotence, e.g., killing everybody, burning up the world, throwing all the people in hell.

C. Empathy. The capacity to view events from the standpoint of others.

Scale Point	Definition of Scale Point
1	No evidence of ability to appreciate other's point of view or needs and feelings. Sees only own needs and not needs or rights of others.
2	Some evidence of ability to appreciate situation from standpoint of another but not enough feeling for other person to convert sympathetic feelings into effective action.
3	Understanding and consideration of other's point of view and/or needs, perhaps resulting in some action or changed behavior.

4   Understanding and consideration of other's needs and
         interests. May move to act on other's behalf whether
         needed or not. May give more than is called for or
         needed. An overresponse.

5   Evidence of identification with those in need. Seems to
         identify with victim and, therefore, cannot appropriately
         assess what is needed; lacks necessary distance or objec-
         tivity. Experiences vicariously the suffering of others.

Appendix 3f

Teacher Questionnaire

Name of Child	Name of Teacher

School	Grade

1. How long has this child been in your classroom? _____
2. How many hours a day is he/she in your classroom? _____
3. Number of children in this class _____

	BELOW AVERAGE	AVERAGE	ABOVE AVERAGE
4. Intelligence			
5. Interest in schoolwork			
6. Attention span			
7. Frustration tolerance			
8. Verbal abilities			
9. Progress in learning			
10. Number of requests for individual help or attention from teacher			

	GENERALLY POSITIVE, ACCEPTING	INDIFFERENT OR VARIABLE	GENERALLY NEGATIVE, DEFIANT
11. Attitude toward adult guidance			
a. In academic work			
b. In non-academic situations			

	LESS THAN MOST	AVERAGE	MORE THAN MOST
12. Shyness			
13. Acceptance by peer group			
a. In the classroom			
b. On the playground			

We are interested in how many children of this age are troubled by the following problems. Are you concerned about this child in any of these areas? Please circle "NO" or "YES" for each question. If "YES," please underline the most appropriate description and explain on the back of this sheet.

14. Have you noticed anything unusual about his/her speech, such as
     a. Groping for the right word?   NO   YES°
     b. Substituting gestures for words?   NO   YES°
     c. Persistent confusion of words?   NO   YES°
     d. Other? Explain.   NO   YES°
     °Please describe and/or give examples.

     CIRCLE ONE:

15. NO   YES   Poor hand coordination in writing, drawing, or manual work
16. NO   YES   Mirror writing, faulty alignment of words, reversal of letters
17. NO   YES   Appearance or action that indicates child may not be well
18. NO   YES   Hyperactivity, inability to sit still in class
19. NO   YES   Extremely irritable
20. NO   YES   Bullying, over aggressive, constantly quarreling
21. NO   YES   Stuttering or stammering
22. NO   YES   Unusual fear or anxiety
23. NO   YES   Destructive
24. NO   YES   Lisping or articulation difficulties
25. NO   YES   Very unhappy, depressed
26. NO   YES   Any nervous habits? Please underline: tics, persistent mannerisms, clearing throat, sniffing, hunching up of shoulders, squinting, twitching of any facial muscles, tapping with feet, nail biting, thumb sucking, other

Thank you for your cooperation.

Additional Comments: _____Over
                       _____None

Note: This questionnaire was adapted from Werner et al. (1971).

Notes

Introduction

1. Findings were reported for the entire group of one-hundred-and-one children and their families in Wittenberg (1971), pp. 343–70.

Chapter 1. The Infant Accident Study

1. All statistical results are based on two-tailed estimates of probability. The acceptable level of probability is .05. In general, t-tests were used to analyze continuous data and chi-square (χ^2) tests to analyze discrete data. In a few instances we did not have responses for the entire sample. By Time Two, five children were living in substitute homes and we could not obtain final data from their mothers.

2. Standards can be found in Appendix 1a.

3. Time One health data for the thirty-four mothers were collected by the pediatrician at the time of the initial evaluation of the infant. The subjects covered in this interview were pregnancy, labor, and delivery of the index child, and acute or chronic conditions affecting the mother, currently or in the past. We also obtained the mother's medical records, including information on pregnancy, labor, and delivery. Mental retardation and emotional problems were noted, although no mother was termed retarded or disturbed without substantial supporting evidence. For the reanalysis two other physicians, blind to the classifications of the mothers, independently evaluated their Time One health in terms of the probable effect on child care. A five-point scale from 1, high risk, to 5, no risk, was used. The Pearson product-moment correlation between the two physicians was .88. For the stability index, each health rating was collapsed into a three-point scale of 0, high risk for child care; 1, moderate risk; and 2, little or no risk.

4. At Time One family stress was assessed by tallying the number of difficulties the mother reported when asked about troublesome events since the conception of the index child. The staff members together categorized the responses, using a modification of Hill's classification (1949). These classifications

had been previously defined and described. In cases of disagreement between the coders, a third staff member resolved the difference.

The number of stress events ranged from zero to sixteen. To make these stress scores comparable with the scoring of other items in the stability index and with the 0–3 scale used at Time Three, they were classified low (score of 3), slight (2), moderate (1), and high (0), using the proportionate distribution of Time Three scores. (The collection of stress data at Time Three is described in chapter 2.)

5. Newberger and Hyde (1975) point out that not only do abusive families lack social support, but they frequently may be victimized by the social institutions charged with helping them (p. 702).

6. Item 3 was evaluated by reviewing the entire Time One–Time Two record for verbalized dissatisfaction with the male. The social-work interviewer and a research assistant made the judgments, using a third person to resolve differences of opinion. In most cases, the mother's information left little room for doubt about her feelings. One mother said, "The only time he isn't criticizing me or banging me around is when he's asleep."

7. The pediatrician who examined the child at both Time One and Time Two rated four aspects of child care. Well-child care and sick-child care were each rated 1, 2, 3, or poor, fair, and good. Immunizations were rated either 1, not complete for age, or 2, satisfactory. Judgment of physical care was based on the child's appearance and cleanliness and the mother's preparations for the hospital visit, for example, provision of extra diapers, a bottle, and toys, and was ranked from 1 to 5, very poor to excellent. The four aspects were considered separately and also as a combined index of infant care.

8. To rate maternal perception, we collected responses to structured items concerning habits, mood, adaptability, persistence, activity, and temperament. At several points during the year's study, we also asked each mother to describe her baby at that time. These responses were classified into the categories of physical development, mental development, health, physical description, and relationships. Two research assistants coded all responses as positive or negative on the basis of carefully defined criteria. (Neutral comments were omitted from the calculations.) We then found the preponderant response, positive or negative, for each mother for each behavioral aspect as well as for all the aspects together.

9. Some mothers were omitted from this calculation, since not all the mothers had scores for every item.

10. The infants were grouped into five developmental levels: significantly slow, slightly slow, normal, slightly advanced, and significantly advanced. We did not rate any baby as deviant from normal unless we had first combined our clinical experience with the test results. Whenever there was a discrepancy, the baby was given the higher rating so as not to risk penalizing him unfairly.

In order to make comparisons between the small groups under consideration, significantly slow and slightly slow were combined, as were slightly advanced and significantly advanced. Rate of development for one year was
assessed for babies who had a Bayley mental score at both Time One and
Time Two. This was calculated by the following formula:

$$\frac{Final\ mental\ score\ minus\ initial\ mental\ score}{Number\ of\ months} \times 12$$

Number of months refers to the elapsed time between the first and final tests.

11. Mood was defined as the amount of pleasant, joyful, friendly behavior
as contrasted with unpleasant, crying, unfriendly behavior and was scored as
positive, variable, or negative. Activity was defined as the level, tempo, and
frequency with which a motor component is present in the child's functioning
(Thomas et al., 1963) and was scored as high, moderate, or low. Distractibility
was defined as the ease with which a child can be induced to give up one
interest for another and was scored as positive or negative.

To keep the conditions of the examination as standardized as possible, the
pediatric evaluation was divided into eight sequences that occurred in the
same order except in the case of a very upset baby. The arrangement of furniture, the seating of individuals, and the lighting were kept the same from one
examination to another.

Prior to the study each behavioral characteristic had been exhaustively
studied and carefully defined. Two observers both simultaneously and independently assessed a number of infants who were not in the study proper.
Then during the study itself, ten infants were scored simultaneously by the
two observers. For each of the three behaviors, interobserver agreement was
estimated by obtaining the proportion of number of agreements to number of
agreements plus disagreements. Estimates of agreement were as follows:
mood, .83; activity, .88; and distractibility, .73.

The measure that was used to compare babies on the behavioral characteristics was the preponderant ratings for each behavior for the whole pediatric
session. This was obtained by calculating the preponderant rating for each
sequence and then combining the sequences to find the overall preponderance.

We are indebted to Alexander Thomas, M.D., for invaluable assistance in
developing this part of the study.

12. This means that 97 percent of children of the same age and sex would
weigh more.

13. Martin et al. (1974) also found that some abused children with positive
neurological signs had no known trauma to the head. This could indicate an
injury so subtle it could not be found on clinical examination or may indicate a
special response to mistreatment.

14. Although the children were no older than two years, it may be significant that these three negative children were black boys and their interviewer was a white woman.

Chapter 2. The Follow-Up Study

1. One of the nineteen abused children was known to be blind because of retinal trauma, a result of abuse. Although she could have been matched to a blind accident child, we did not include her in the study, for when the interviewers visited the home, the child was found incapable of speech, comprehension, or ambulation because of extreme brain damage. No useful purpose would have been served by including her as she could not have responded to any of the procedures. Later, one mother in the abuse group decided not to bring her child for evaluation.

2. We are greatly indebted to the Child Welfare Services of Allegheny, Beaver, and Fayette Counties for assistance in locating five foster and three adoptive families and eliciting their cooperation.

3. It may be assumed that these substitute homes were chosen because they offered greater stability and support and better child care practices. Thus, these families would more resemble the accident and comparison families than the natural abusive families.

4. Standards can be found in Appendix 2b.

5. Information was gathered by the interviewers and, as for the Time One–Time Two data, independently rated by two physicians who were blind to the classification of the mothers. The Pearson product-moment correlation between the judges for the fifty-nine women was .77. In cases of disagreement, the final rating was the result of a forced consensus. For the stability index, the five-point ratings were collapsed to a scale of 0, high risk for child care; 1, moderate risk; and 2, no risk.

6. A rough gauge of family stress at Time Three was obtained by the mother's responses to the following questions: (1) What kinds of difficult situations have come up when you've needed help in the past year? (From the home interview schedule.) (2) Have there been any recent changes (e.g., death, job change, a move) in the family's way of life? (3) Is the family struggling with any major problems? (Numbers 2 and 3 are from the pediatric history interview.) Each item was scored either 0, no difficult situation, no recent change, no major problem, or 1. When more than one problem was mentioned in one response, the score remained 1. On the other hand, if the mother mentioned the same problem in each item, it was scored separately for each, as a repeated response seemed to indicate greater concern. In case of financial problems because of dependence on welfare, a score of 0 was given, as adequate income was another item in the index. However, a financial crisis due to loss of a job or unforeseen medical expenses was given a score of 1.

For the stability index, stress scores were summed and reversed: i.e., a mother who reported no problems in any response received a final score of 3, while a mother who reported positively in each item had a score of 0.

7. Continuity of child care was assessed by inquiring whether the natural mother had had the child without interruption since birth, or whether the foster or adoptive mother had had the child without interruption since the initial placement.

8. The husband or boyfriend was scored 2 for any specific help given and all others were scored 1 except for children under eighteen, who were scored .5. Types of supportive activities were classified as household management (cleaning, cooking, yard help, repair, etc.), confide/talk, child care, help with transportation, and assistance with family problems. Each activity was scored as 1 except for confide/talk, which received 2. Help of an unspecified kind was scored as .5.

A source of potential bias was the propensity of some mothers to give greater detail than others. The solution was to score each type of resource only once for each type of activity. Thus, if a mother described several aunts and cousins who would baby-sit, she received only a score of 1 in the "Care of children" row under "Other Relatives."

The assigned value of the resource was multiplied by the value of the function. The sum of these products, to which was added one point for a male partner living in the home, was the support score for the individual mother.

9. Ratings were 1, unsatisfactory, or 2, satisfactory, for immunizations and for dental care. The physical appearance of children of this age was judged less important for health than the physical appearance of an infant. This aspect therefore was rated 0 for unsatisfactory and 1 for satisfactory. The items were analyzed separately and then combined into a child care index with a range of 2 to 5.

10. A miscellaneous category was used for other offenses considered punishable by the mother but not itemized on the interview. Two judges jointly scored several children who were not part of the study proper to develop the criteria for rating. The study cases were then rated independently by each judge, and the percentage of concordance was found by calculating the number of occurrences agreed upon compared with the total number of occurrences (the mean of both observers' tallies). This formula eliminated absence of a category as a factor in calculating concordance. Concordance for the ten cases ranged from .67 to .97 with a mean of .86. Since we found that some of the responses were most inappropriate, tallies were also made of inappropriate maternal reactions.

11. Criteria were set up for each of these categories, along with many examples for each. Two judges reviewed cases for three children not in the study proper, exchanging information and ideas about how to rate the comments. They then judged ten study cases independently and assessed reliability by

calculating the number of agreements over the number of agreements plus disagreements. For the ten cases, each averaging twenty-six items, the mean reliability was .84. The raw scores for positive, negative, and neutral were then converted into proportions of the mother's total comments about the child in order to avoid handicapping the nonverbal mothers.

12. The questionnaire "Your Child — Most Children" was modeled on the inventory of neonatal perception described in Broussard and Hartner (1971). The mother rated her child on ten items, using a five-point scale. She then rated other children of similar age on the same items, according to what she thought they might be like. Each item was analyzed to find the proportion of mothers in each group who rated their children worse than others versus the proportion who rated their children better. Ties were disregarded.

13. The system of measuring support was different at Time Three than at Time One. We subtracted the individual score of the child's caretaker at Time One from the score of the caretaker at Time Three. The statistical test was applied to the difference between the two scores.

14. Each aspect was scored on a five-point scale from 1, very poor, to 5, excellent, on the basis of the physician's written findings. Criteria for scoring were specifically defined and examples were provided. In assessing the first two of the five aspects, consideration was given to (1) probable occurrence in a given age group, (2) long-term effects, (3) reason (if given), and (4) frequency. A collection of related symptoms within or among systems was considered in rating systems review. The neurological rating was based on presence or absence of abnormality of cranial nerve function, motor system coordination, deep tendon reflexes, and sensory system.

15. All the child's productions were tape-recorded. Articulation during conversation was scored from the tapes, and expressive language from the transcripts. For each of the three evaluations of language, a five-point scale from very poor to very good was used.

Test-retest reliability of judgments on articulation during conversation was assessed by repeat judgments two months later. A research assistant selected the tapes, from which the names had been removed, of twelve children, two from each group (abuse, accident, comparison) with high scores and two with low. These tapes were judged a second time and the test-retest reliability was .89. The same procedure was employed for test-retest reliability of judgments on expressive language, using the transcripts of twelve other children. Test-retest reliability was .96.

Reliability of the judgments was assessed by comparing the examiner's results with those of two other speech pathologists who made independent judgments of articulation and expressive language on the same twenty-four children. Reliability figures were .88 and .90 for articulation and the same for expressive language. During the presentation of the above items, the examiner also studied other aspects of the child's communication. Particularly noted were such problems as excessive lack of fluency, stuttering, and voice deviations. Impressions regarding these problems were noted on the protocols during the examination.

At a later time mean length of utterance was calculated in order to furnish a more objective measure of linguistic complexity than that supplied by the linguistic judgments. Brown (1973) suggests that the mean length of utterance is an excellent simple index of grammatical development because almost every new kind of linguistic knowledge increases length. To obtain this measure, the guidelines set forth by Brown were followed except for the elimination of one count that might have handicapped users of black dialect. The overall mean length of utterance was based on transcriptions of the responses to the Blacky pictures and of the child's five stories as related to the speech pathologist.

16. Three judges, all experienced in expressive arts and all trained in the use of the rating system, were employed. A pair of judges, working independently, rated each characteristic. Three hundred fifty-four stories (six for each of the fifty-nine subjects) were rated for each of the three traits. Reliability figures were as follows: impulsivity, .83; aggression, .98; and empathy, .97.

The groups of children were compared as to the mean score of each behavioral quality for each story and across all stories, and as to the difference between judgments for story 5 minus story 1 and story 6 minus story 1 for each behavior, using an analysis of variance. This was to assess possible increase or decrease in impulsivity and aggression as the child got into increasing amounts of fantasy material. Repeated measures analysis of variance was used to assess changes in pattern between groups.

17. This is a paper-and-pencil test yielding numerical scores of self-concept in relation to six areas: behavior, intelligence, physical appearance, anxiety, popularity, and happiness. In addition, there is an overall score, the sum of the six subscales.

18. For further information concerning the assessment of motor activity in traumatized children, contact the author, Parental Stress Center, 918 S. Negley Avenue, Pittsburgh, Pa. 15232.

19. Each item of the pre-coded teacher questionnaire was analyzed separately by assigning a numerical score. In general, teacher ratings of below average, less than most, or a negative comment received a 0; a rating of average or a neutral comment received a 1; and above average, more than most, or a positive comment received a 2. The presence of a negative behavioral trait or a communication difficulty received a 0; absence of the trait was scored 1. Total scores were added to find the teacher's overall impression of each child.

20. This procedure involves the application of two-population Bayes decision rules based on discrete data. A step-wise procedure selects the predictor variables most closely associated with each child outcome. The program yields the percentage of the sample that is correctly predicted by various patterns of the predictor variables. The nine child-outcome variables were dichotomized

and submitted to this analysis, using forty possible predictor variables, which were also dichotomized. Each of the nine outcomes was compared with the forty predictor variables to identify fruitful associations for later analysis. As can be seen, this is a relatively gross procedure designed to produce leads for further, more refined investigation.

21. Friedman and Morse (1974) reported a study carried out in 1970–1971 designed to test the reliability of judgments concerning abuse, neglect, and accidents. At the time of their follow-up, five years after the initial study, the original judgments were changed in 15 percent of the cases, a figure similar to ours, which was 20 percent. One could, of course, look at the doughnut instead of the hole and say that from 80 to 85 percent of the judgments were confirmed in both investigations. This seems to beg the issue with respect to the families and children who were misclassified and may therefore have endured a different kind of abuse at the hands of well-intentioned persons.

Bibliography

Anderson, C.
1972   Screening the hearing of preschool and school age children. In *Handbook of Clinical Audiology*, ed. J. Katz. Baltimore: Williams and Wilkins Company.

Baher, E.; Hyman, C.; Jones, C.; Jones, R.; Kerr, A.; and Mitchell, R.
1976   *At Risk: An Account of the Work of the Battered Child Research Department, National Society for the Prevention of Cruelty to Children.* London: Routledge & Kegan Paul Ltd.

Baldwin, J. A., and Oliver, J. E.
1975   Epidemiology and family characteristics of severely-abused children. *British Journal of Preventive and Social Medicine* 29:205–21.

Baughman, E. E.
1971   *Black Americans: A Psychological Analysis.* New York: Academic Press, Inc.

Bayley, N.
1965   Comparisons of mental and motor test scores for ages 1–15 months by sex, birth order, race, geographical location, and education of parents. *Child Development* 36:379–411.

Bayley, N.
1969   *Bayley Scales of Infant Development.* New York: The Psychological Corporation.

Bernard, J.
1974   *The Future of Motherhood.* New York: The Dial Press.

Bernstein, B.
1959   A public language: some sociological implications of a linguistic form. *The British Journal of Sociology* 10:311–26.

Birch, H. G., and Gussow, J. D.
1970   *Disadvantaged Children: Health, Nutrition and School Failure.* New York: Grune & Stratton, Inc.

Birch, H. G., and Richardson, S. A.
    1972 The functioning of Jamaican school children severely malnour-
          ished during the first two years of life. In *Nutrition, the Nervous
          System, and Behavior*. Scientific publication no. 251. Washington,
          D.C.: Pan American Health Organization.
Blum, G. S.
    1950 *The Blacky Pictures: A Technique for the Exploration of Person-
          ality Dynamics*. Ann Arbor: Psychodynamic Instruments.
Bowlby, J.
    1969 *Attachment and Loss*. Vol 1. New York: Basic Books, Inc.
Broussard, E. R., and Hartner, M. S. S.
    1971 Further considerations regarding maternal perception of the first
          born. In *Exceptional Infant*, ed. J. Hellmuth. Vol. 2. New York:
          Brunner/Mazel, Inc.
Brown, R. W.
    1973 *A First Language: The Early Stages*. Cambridge, Mass.: Harvard
          University Press.
Caffey, J.
    1946 Multiple fractures in the long bones of infants suffering from
          chronic subdural hematoma. *The American Journal of Roentgen-
          ology and Radium Therapy* 56:163–73.
Cattell, P.
    1960 *Cattell Infant Intelligence Scale*. New York: The Psychological
          Corporation.
Church, J.
    1961 *Language and the Discovery of Reality: A Developmental Psy-
          chology of Cognition*. New York: Random House, Inc.
Coleman, J. S., et al.
    1966 *Equality of Educational Opportunity*. Washington, D.C.: U. S.
          Government Printing Office.
Davie, R.
    1973 Eleven years of childhood. In *Statistical News: Developments in
          British Official Statistics*. London: Her Majesty's Stationery Office.
Duncan, S.; Young, M.; and Kirkwood, M.
    1974 Education. In *Poverty Report 1974*, ed. M. Young. London:
          Maurice Temple Smith, Ltd.
Ebbin, A. J.; Gollub, M. H.; Stein, A. M.; and Wilson, M. G.
    1969 Battered child syndrome at Los Angeles County General Hospital.
          American Journal of Diseases of Children 118:660–67.
Ekstein, R.
    1965 Puppet play of a psychotic adolescent girl in the psychothera-
          peutic process. In *The Psychoanalytic Study of the Child*, ed. R. S.
          Eissler, A. Freud, H. Hartmann, and M. Kris. Vol. 20. New York:
          International Universities Press, Inc.

Elmer, E.
   1967   *Children in Jeopardy.* Pittsburgh: University of Pittsburgh Press.
Evans, S. L.; Reinhart, J. B.; and Succop, R. A.
   1972   Failure to thrive: a study of forty-five children and their families. *The Journal of The American Academy of Child Psychiatry* 11: 440–57.
Farber, B.
   1968   *Mental Retardation: Its Social Context and Social Consequences.* Boston: Houghton Mifflin Company.
Fontana, V. J.
   1973   *Somewhere a Child Is Crying: Maltreatment — Causes and Prevention.* New York: Macmillan Publishing Company, Inc.
Friedman, S. B., and Morse, C. W.
   1974   Child abuse: a five-year follow-up of early case finding in the emergency department. *Pediatrics* 54:404–10.
Fudala, J.
   1970   *Arizona Articulation Proficiency Scale, Revised.* Los Angeles: Western Psychological Services.
Galdston, R.
   1965   Observations on children who have been physically abused and their parents. *The American Journal of Psychiatry* 122:440–43.
Galdston, R.
   1971   Violence begins at home. *The Journal of The American Academy of Child Psychiatry* 10:336–50.
Gibbens, T. C. N., and Walker, A.
   1956   *Cruel Parents.* London: The Institute for the Study and Treatment of Delinquency.
Gil, D. G.
   1970   *Violence Against Children: Physical Child Abuse in the United States.* Cambridge, Mass.: Harvard University Press.
Ginsburg, H.
   1972   *The Myth of the Deprived Child: Poor Children's Intellect and Education.* Englewood Cliffs, N. J.: Prentice-Hall, Inc.
Goldfarb, W.
   1945   Effects of psychological deprivation in infancy and subsequent stimulation. *The American Journal of Psychiatry* 102:18–33.
Greenberg, N. H.
   1970   Atypical behavior during infancy: infant development in relation to the behavior and personality of the mother. In *The Child and His Family*, ed. E. J. Anthony and C. Koupernik. Vol 1. New York: John Wiley & Sons.
Gregg, G. S., and Elmer, E.
   1969   Infant injuries: accident or abuse? *Pediatrics* 44:434–39.

Haworth, M. R.
  1968 Doll play and puppetry. In *Projective Techniques in Personality Assessment,* ed. A. I. Rabin. New York: Springer Publishing Company, Inc.
Herzog, E., and Sudia, C. E.
  1973 Children in fatherless families. In *Review of Child Development Research,* ed. B. M. Caldwell and H. N. Ricciuti. Vol. 3. Chicago: The University of Chicago Press.
Hill, R.
  1949 *Families Under Stress.* New York: Harper and Bros.
Hobbs, N.
  1976 *Mental Health, Families, and Children.* Austin, Tex.: University of Texas Printing Division.
Hollingshead, A. B.
  1957 *Two Factor Index of Social Position.* Privately printed, 1965, Yale Station, New Haven, Conn. For a discussion of the scale see J. K. Myers and L. L. Bean, 1968, *A Decade Later: A Follow-Up of Social Class and Mental Illness.* New York: John Wiley and Sons, Inc.
Holman, R. R., and Kanwar, S.
  1975 Early life of the "battered child." *Archives of Disease in Childhood* 50:78–80.
Holmes, T. H., and Rahe, R. H.
  1967 The social readjustment rating scale. *Journal of Psychosomatic Research* 11:213–18.
Irwin, E., and Shapiro, M.
  1975 Puppetry as a diagnostic and therapeutic tool. In *Psychiatry and Art,* ed. I. Jakab. Vol. 4. Basel, Switzerland: S. Karger.
Jenkins, S.
  1974 Child welfare as a class system. In *Children and Decent People,* ed. A. L. Schorr. New York: Basic Books, Inc.
Justice, B., and Duncan, D. F.
  1976 Life crisis as a precursor to child abuse. *Public Health Reports* 91:110–15.
Kempe, C. H.
  1976 Approaches to preventing child abuse: the health visitors concept. *American Journal of Diseases of Children* 130:941–47.
Kempe, C. H.; Silverman, F. N.; Steele, B. F.; Droegemueller, W.; and Silver, H. K.
  1962 The battered-child syndrome. *The Journal of the American Medical Association* 181:17–24.
Klein, M., and Stern, L.
  1971 Low birth weight and the battered child syndrome. *American Journal of Diseases of Children* 122:15–18.

Koel, B. S.
    1969   Failure to thrive and fatal injury as a continuum. *American Journal of Diseases of Children* 118:565–67.
Koppitz, E. M.
    1964   *The Bender Gestalt Test for Young Children.* New York: Grune & Stratton, Inc.
Korsch, B. M.; Christian, J. B.; Gozzi, E. K.; and Carlson, P. V.
    1965   Infant care and punishment: a pilot study. *American Journal of Public Health* 55:1880–88.
Krogman, W. M.
    1970   Growth of head, face, trunk, and limbs in Philadelphia white and Negro children of elementary and high school age. *Monographs of the Society for Research in Child Development.* Vol. 35, serial no. 136, no. 3.
Lachin, J. M.
    1973   On a stepwise procedure for two population Bayes decision rules using discrete variables. *Biometrics* 29:551–64.
Lampkin, L. C.
    1971   Alienation as a coping mechanism: "out where the action is." In *Crises of Family Disorganization,* ed. E. Pavenstedt and V. W. Bernard. New York: Behavioral Publications.
Lesser, G. S.; Fifer, G.; and Clark, D. H.
    1965   Mental abilities of children from different social-class and cultural groups. *Monographs of the Society for Research in Child Development.* Vol. 30, serial no. 102, no. 4.
Light, R. J.
    1973   Abused and neglected children in America: a study of alternative policies. *Harvard Educational Review* 43:556–98.
Mahler, M. S.
    1968   *On Human Symbiosis and the Vicissitudes of Individuation: Infantile Psychosis.* Vol. 1. New York: International Universities Press, Inc.
Mahler, M. S., and Furer, M.
    1963   Certain aspects of the separation-individuation phase. *The Psychoanalytic Quarterly* 32:1–14.
Martin, H. P.; Beezley, P.; Conway, E. F.; and Kempe, C. H.
    1974   The development of abused children. In *Advances in Pediatrics,* ed. I. Schulman. Vol. 21. Chicago: Year Book Medical Publishers, Inc.
Morse, C. W.; Sahler, O. J. Z.; and Friedman, S. B.
    1970   A three year follow-up study of abused and neglected children. *American Journal of Diseases of Children* 120:439–46.

Newberger, E. H., and Hyde, J. N., Jr.
1975   Child abuse: principles and implications of current pediatric practice. *The Pediatric Clinics of North America* 22:695–715.

Owens, D. J., and Straus, M. A.
1975   The social structure of violence in childhood and approval of violence as an adult. *Aggressive Behavior* 1:193–211.

Patton, R. G., and Gardner, L. I.
1963   *Growth Failure in Maternal Deprivation.* Springfield, Ill.: Charles C Thomas.

Pavenstedt, E.
1971   The meanings of motherhood in a deprived community. In *Crises of Family Disorganization*, ed. E. Pavenstedt and V. W. Bernard. New York: Behavioral Publications.

Piers, E. V., and Harris, D. B.
1970   *The Piers-Harris Children's Self Concept Scale.* Nashville: Counselor Recordings and Tests.

Pollock, C., and Steele, B.
1972   A therapeutic approach to the parents. In *Helping the Battered Child and His Family*, ed. C. H. Kempe and R. E. Helfer. Philadelphia: J. B. Lippincott Company.

Provence, S., and Lipton, R. C.
1962   *Infants in Institutions: A Comparison of Their Development with Family-Reared Infants During the First Year of Life.* New York: International Universities Press, Inc.

Radbill, S. X.
1968   A history of child abuse and infanticide. In *The Battered Child*, ed. R. E. Helfer and C. H. Kempe. Chicago: The University of Chicago Press.

Rambert, M. L.
1949   *Children in Conflict: Twelve Years of Psychoanalytic Practice.* New York: International Universities Press, Inc.

Richardson, S. A.
1972   Ecology of malnutrition: nonnutritional factors influencing intellectual and behavioral development. In *Nutrition, the Nervous System, and Behavior.* Scientific publication no. 251. Washington, D.C.: Pan American Health Organization.

Richardson, S. A.; Birch, H. G.; and Hertzig, M. E.
1973   School performance of children who were severely malnourished in infancy. *American Journal of Mental Deficiency* 77:623–32.

Rodham, H.
1973   Children under the law. *Harvard Educational Review* 43:487–514. Quotes S. Kessler, unpublished paper on past White House Conferences on Children (New Haven, Conn.: Carnegie Council on Children, 1972).

Sandgrund, A.; Gaines, R. W.; and Green, A. H.
1974   Child abuse and mental retardation: a problem of cause and effect. *American Journal of Mental Deficiency* 79:327–30.
Schneider, C.; Pollock, C.; and Helfer, R. E.
1972   Interviewing the parents. In *Helping the Battered Child and His Family,* ed. C. H. Kempe and R. E. Helfer. Philadelphia: J. B. Lippincott Company.
Schneider, C.; Hoffmeister, J. K.; and Helfer, R. E.
1976   A predictive screening questionnaire for potential problems in mother-child interaction. In *Child Abuse and Neglect: The Family and the Community,* ed. R. E. Helfer and C. H. Kempe. Cambridge, Mass.: Ballinger Publishing Company.
Schorr, A. L., ed.
1974   *Children and Decent People.* New York: Basic Books, Inc.
Silver, A., and Hagin, R.
1972   Profile of a first grade: a basis for preventive psychiatry. *The Journal of The American Academy of Child Psychiatry* 11:645–74.
Silver, L. B.; Dublin, C. C.; and Lourie, R. S.
1969   Does violence breed violence? Contributions from a study of the child abuse syndrome. *The American Journal of Psychiatry* 126: 404–07.
Silverman, F. N.
1953   The roentgen manifestations of unrecognized skeletal trauma in infants. *American Journal of Roentgenology Radium Therapy and Nuclear Medicine* 69:413–27.
Smith, J. M.
1974   Incidence of atopic disease. *Medical Clinics of North America* 58:3–24.
Sobel, R.
1973   "What went right?": the natural history of the early traumatized. In *Interpersonal Explorations in Psychoanalysis,* ed. E. G. Witenberg. New York: Basic Books, Inc.
Spitz, R. A.
1945   Hospitalism: an inquiry into the genesis of psychiatric conditions in early childhood. In *The Psychoanalytic Study of the Child,* ed. A. Freud, H. Hartmann, and E. Kris. Vol. 1. New York: International Universities Press, Inc.
Stuart, H. C., and Stevenson, S. S.
1950   Physical growth and development. In *Mitchell-Nelson Textbook of Pediatrics,* ed. W. E. Nelson. 5th ed. Philadelphia: W. B. Saunders Company.
Sussman, A., and Cohen, S. J.
1975   *Reporting Child Abuse and Neglect: Guidelines for Legislation.* Cambridge, Mass.: Ballinger Publishing Company.

Terman, L., and Merrill, M.
    1960   *The Stanford-Binet Intelligence Scale: Third Revision, Form L-M.* Boston: Houghton Mifflin Company.

Terr, L. C.
    1970   A family study of child abuse. *The American Journal of Psychiatry.* 127:125–31.

Thomas, A. B.; Chess, S.; Birch, H. G.; Hertzig, M.; and Korn, S.
    1963   *Behavioral Individuality in Early Childhood.* New York: New York University Press.

Werner, E.; Simonian, K.; Bierman, J. M.; and French, F. E.
    1967   Cumulative effect of perinatal complications and deprived environment on physical, intellectual and social development of preschool children. *Pediatrics* 39:490–505.

Werner, E. E.; Bierman, J. M.; and French, F. E.
    1971   *The Children of Kauai: A Longitudinal Study from the Prenatal Period to Age Ten.* Honolulu: University of Hawaii Press.

Wittenberg, C.
    1971   Studies of child abuse and infant accidents. In *The Mental Health of the Child: Program Reports of the National Institute of Mental Health,* ed. J. Segal. Washington, D.C.: U. S. Government Printing Office.

Woltmann, A. G.
    1940   The use of puppets in understanding children. *Mental Hygiene* 24:445–58.

Woltmann, A. G.
    1960   Spontaneous puppetry by children as a projective method. In *Projective Techniques with Children,* ed. A. I. Rabin and M. R. Haworth. New York: Grune & Stratton, Inc.

Woolley, P. V., Jr., and Evans, W. A., Jr.
    1955   Significance of skeletal lesions in infants resembling those of traumatic origin. *The Journal of the American Medical Association* 158:539–43.

Index

Contemporary Community Health Series

MARRIAGE AND MENTAL HANDICAP:
A Study of Subnormality in Marriage
Janet Mattinson

A METHOD OF HOSPITAL UTILIZATION REVIEW
Sidney Shindell and Morris London

METHODOLOGY IN EVALUATING THE QUALITY
OF MEDICAL CARE: *An Annotated Selected Bibliography, 1955–1968*
Isidore Altman, Alice J. Anderson, and Kathleen Barker
Out of print

MIGRANTS AND MALARIA IN AFRICA
R. Mansell Prothero
Out of print

A PSYCHIATRIC RECORD MANUAL FOR THE HOSPITAL
Dorothy Smith Keller

RACISM AND MENTAL HEALTH
Charles V. Willie, Bernard M. Kramer, and Bertram S. Brown, Editors

THE SOCIOLOGY OF PHYSICAL DISABILITY AND REHABILITATION
Gary L. Albrecht, Editor

THE STYLE AND MANAGEMENT OF A PEDIATRIC PRACTICE
Lee W. Bass and Jerome H. Wolfson

DATE DUE